C000318566

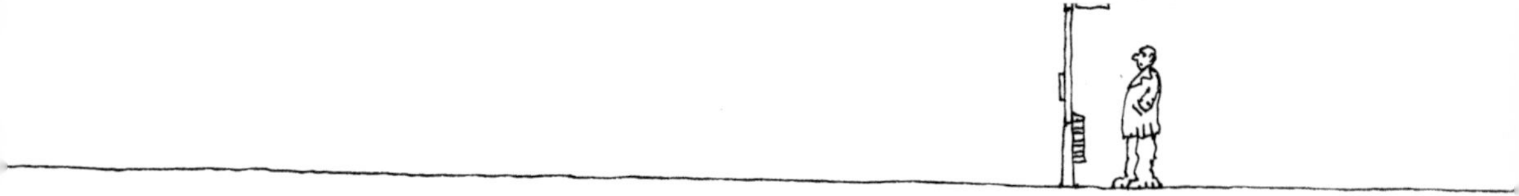

'Commuter – one who spends his life
In riding to and from his wife;
A man who shaves and takes a train
And then rides back to shave again.'

*E B White*

# Simon Bond

## COMMUTED TO LIFE

### *Humour to get you home*

Silver Link Publishing Ltd

© Simon Bond 1992

All rights reserved. No part of this publication may be reproduced, stored in a retrieval system or transmitted, in any form or by any means, electronic, mechanical, photocopying, recording or otherwise, without prior permission in writing from Silver Link Publishing Ltd.

First published in April 1992
Reprinted September 1992

British Library Cataloguing in Publication Data

Bond, Simon
Commuted to Life: Humour to Get You Home
I. Title
388

ISBN 0 947971 91 2

Silver Link Publishing Ltd
Unit 5
Home Farm Close
Church Street
Wadenhoe
Peterborough PE8 5TE
Tel/fax: (08015) 4-4-0

Printed and bound in Great Britain by Woolnough Bookbinding Ltd, Irthlingborough, Northants

# THE FIRST COMMUTERS

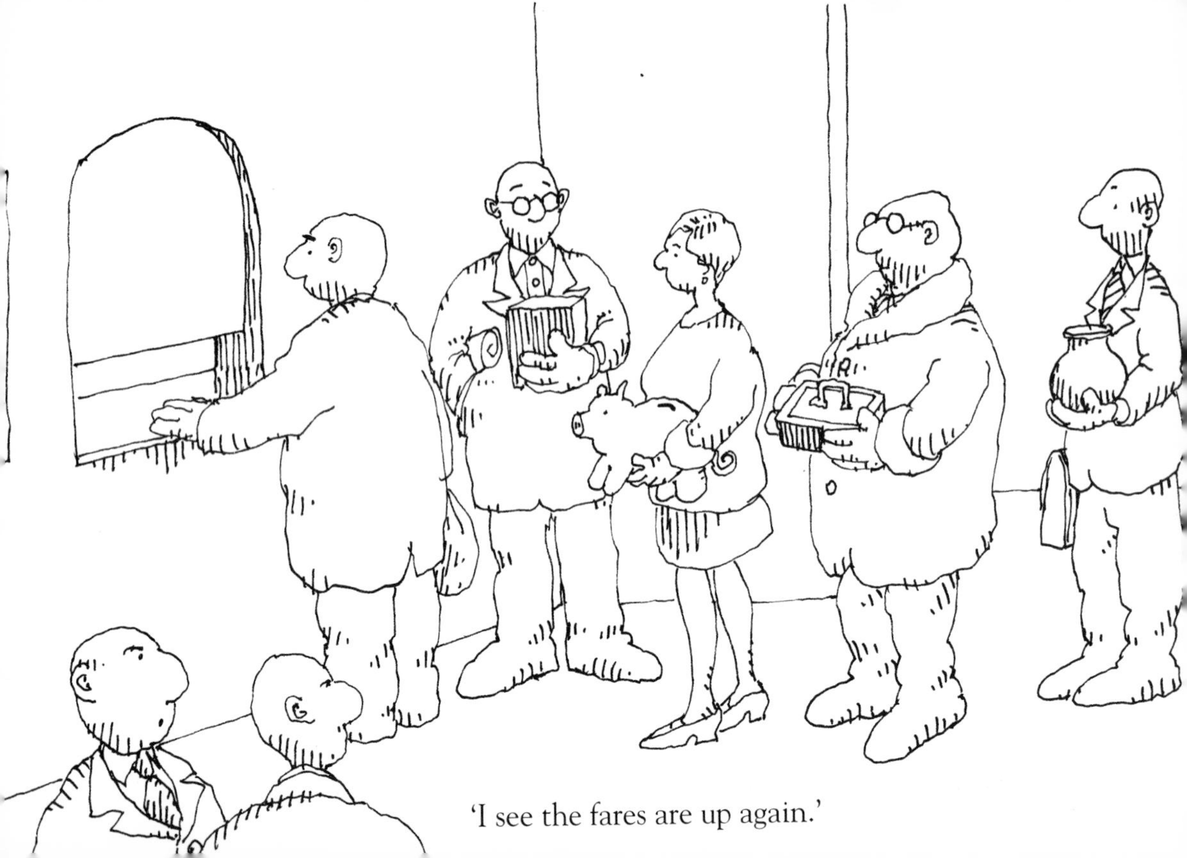

'I see the fares are up again.'

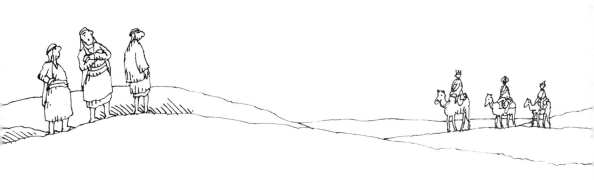

'Bloody typical . . . you wait for ever then three of the buggers come along together!'

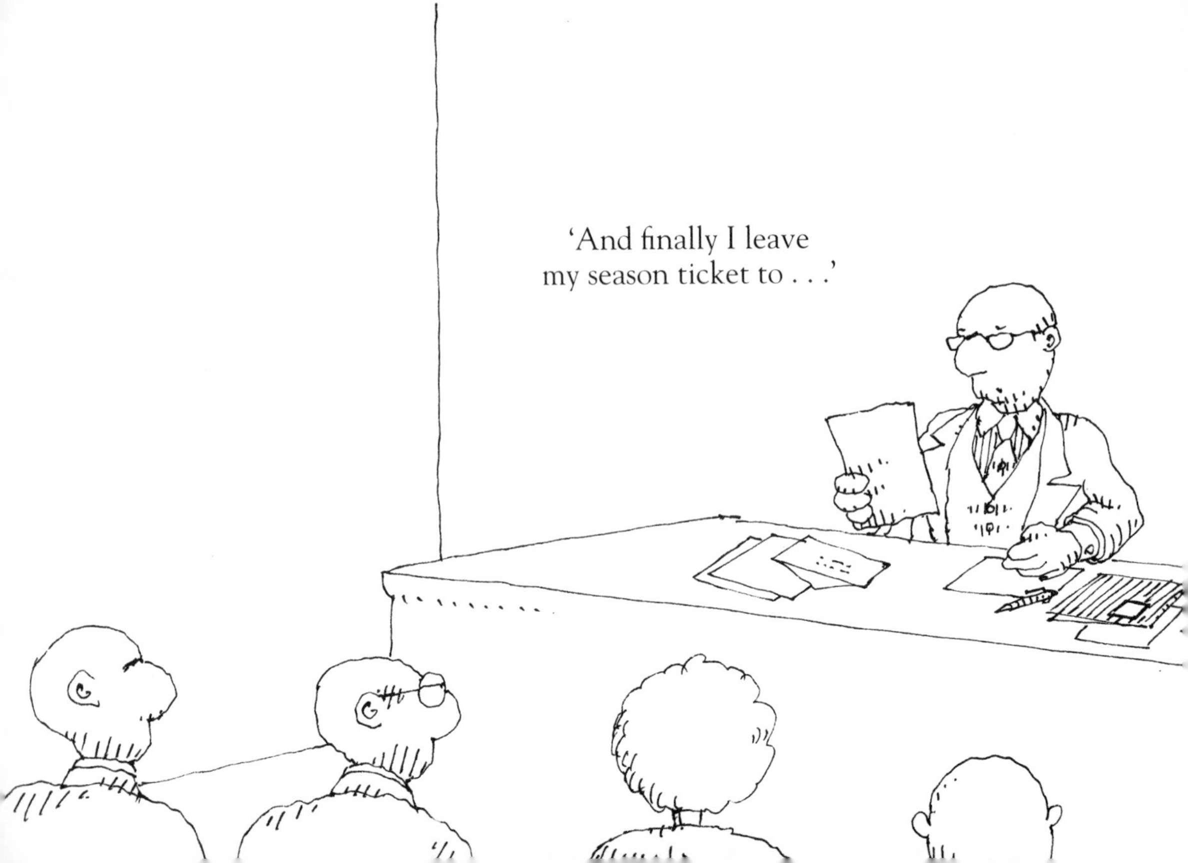

'And finally I leave
my season ticket to . . .'

THE GOVT. BEGINS TO PUMP MONEY INTO TRANSPORT

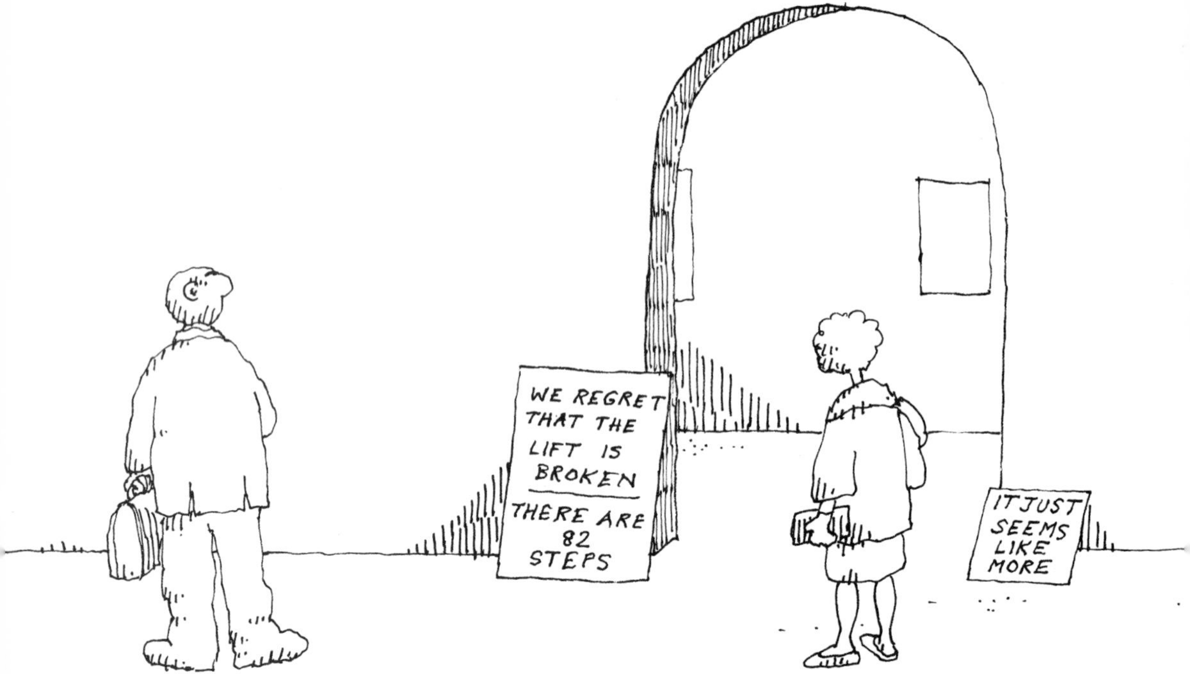
WE REGRET THAT THE LIFT IS BROKEN
THERE ARE 82 STEPS
IT JUST SEEMS LIKE MORE

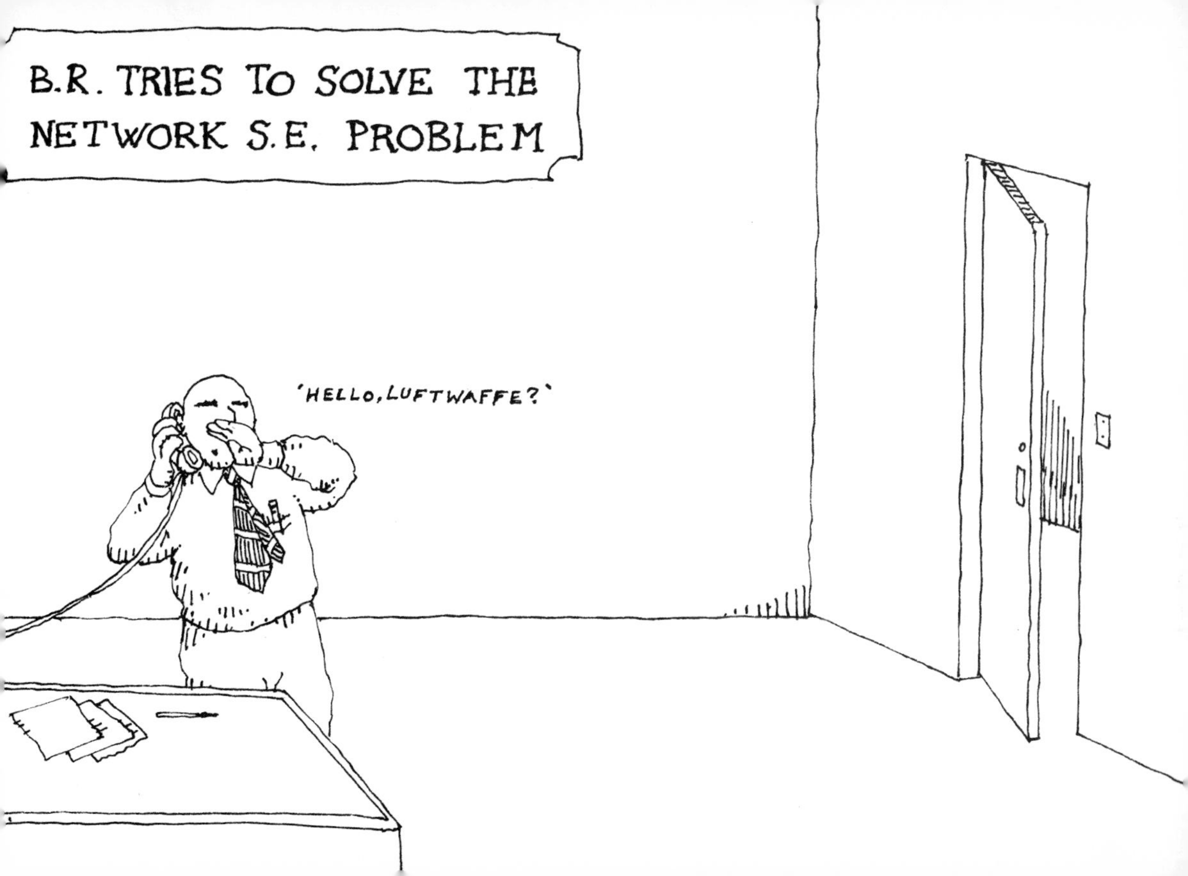
B.R. TRIES TO SOLVE THE NETWORK S.E. PROBLEM
'HELLO, LUFTWAFFE?'

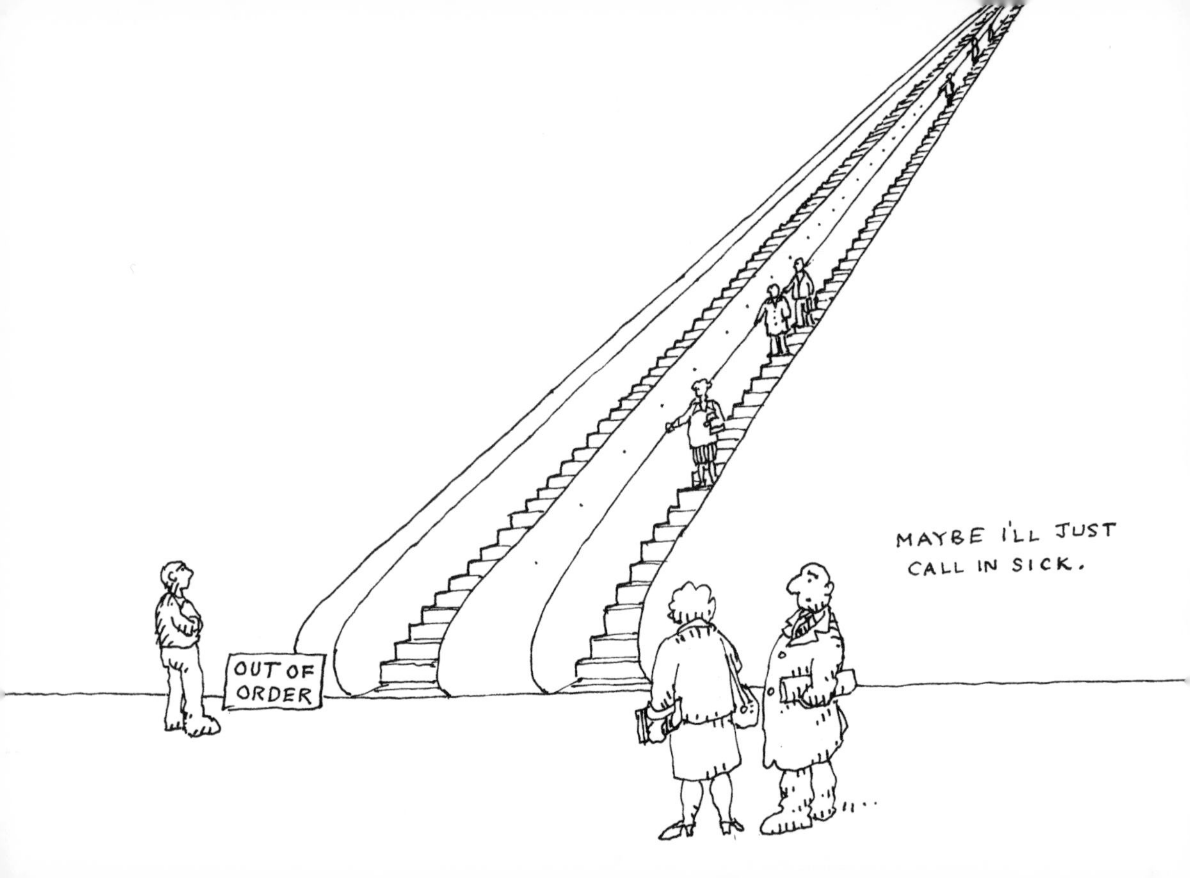
MAYBE I'LL JUST
CALL IN SICK.
OUT OF
ORDER

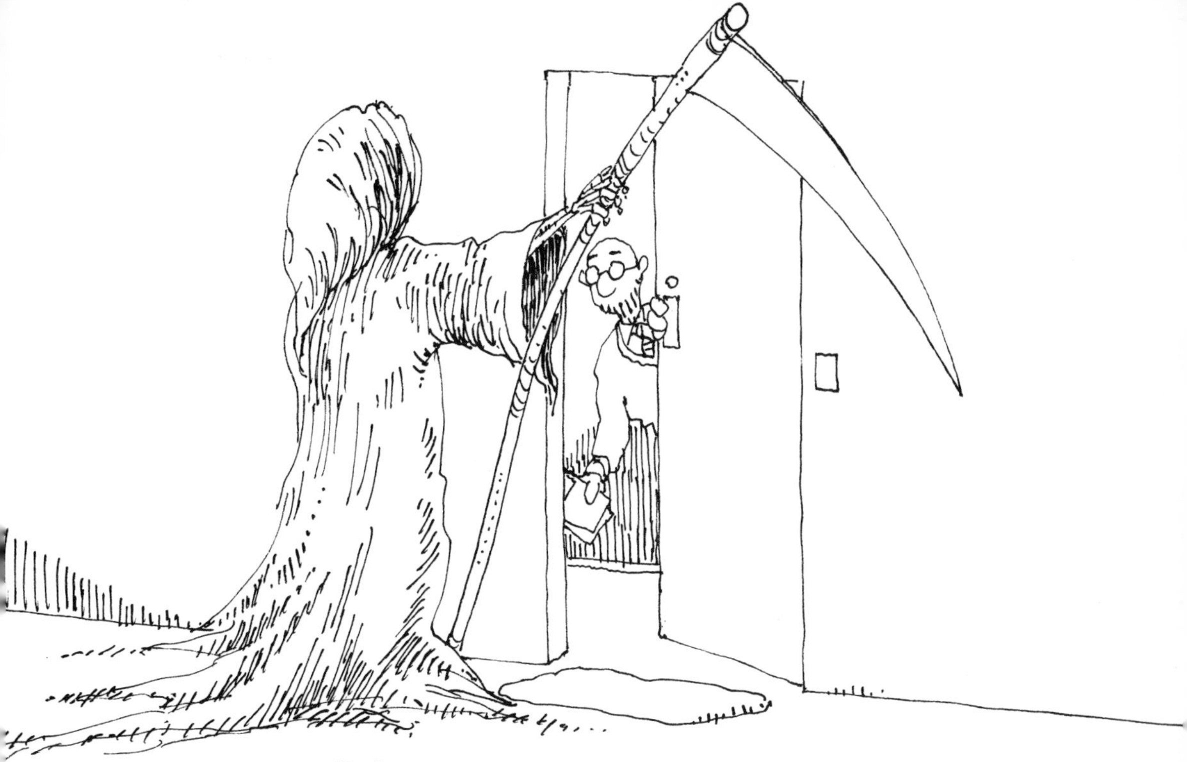

'Relax . . . I've come for your bus pass.'

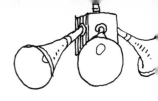

WE APOLOGIZE FOR THE LATE ARRIVAL
OF THE 1945 TRAIN..... STARRING
TREVOR HOWARD AND CELIA JOHNSON....

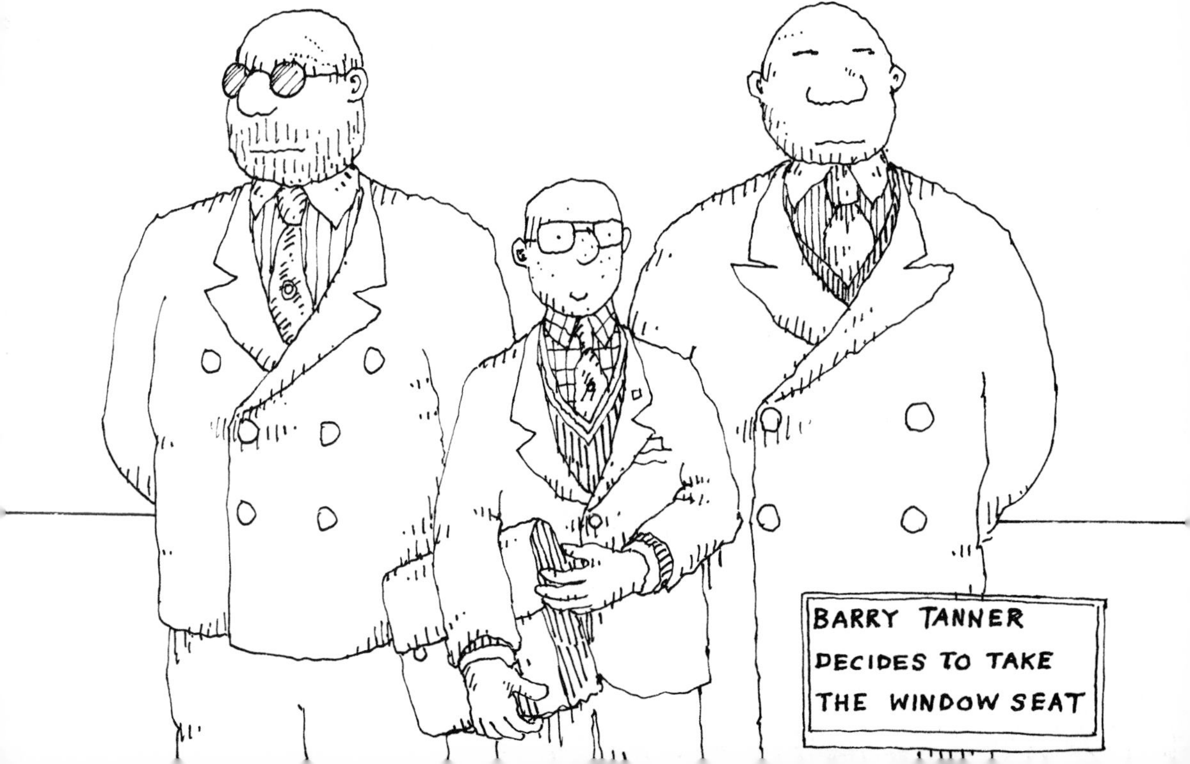
BARRY TANNER
DECIDES TO TAKE
THE WINDOW SEAT

# *Old Habits Die Hard*

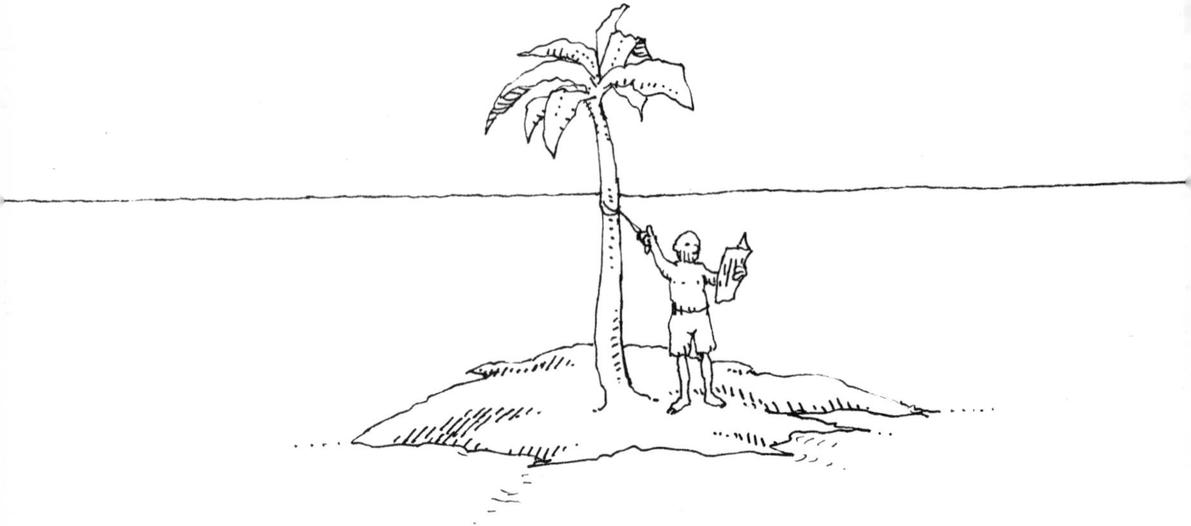

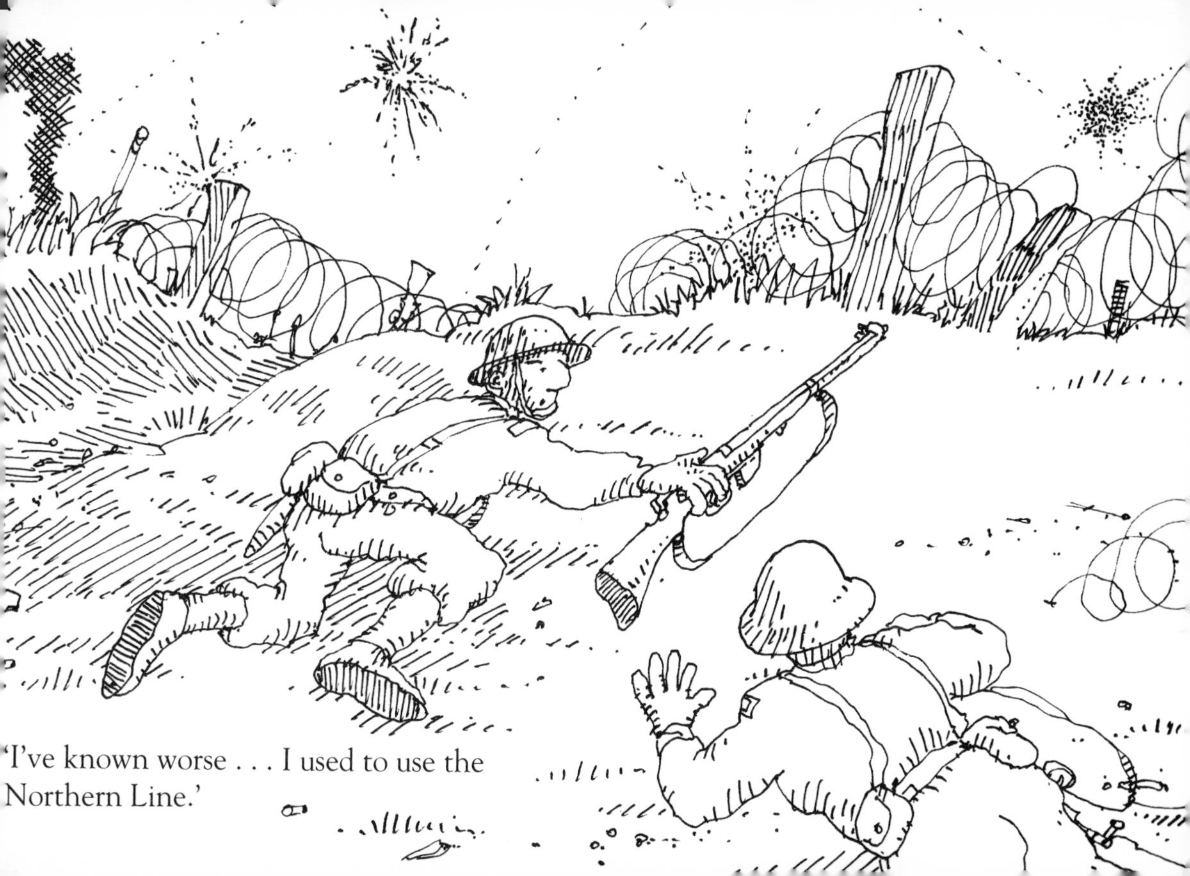

'I've known worse . . . I used to use the Northern Line.'

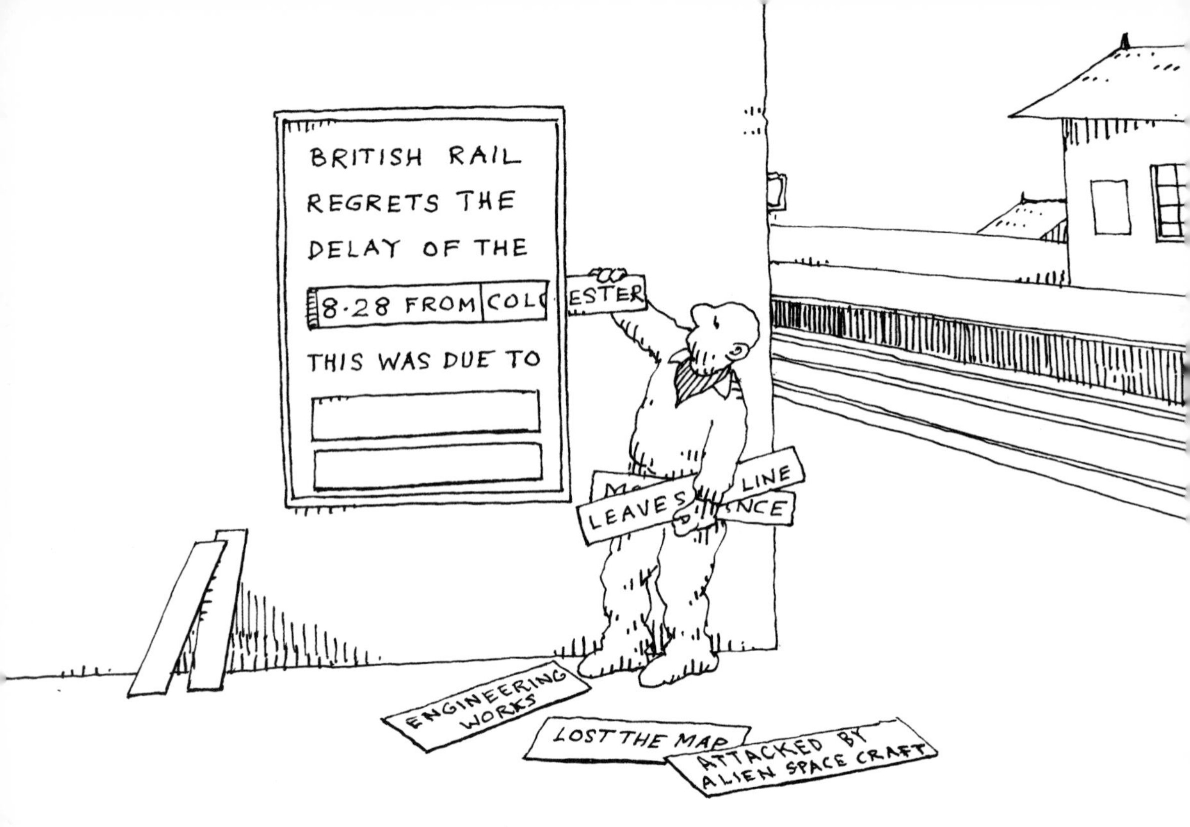

BRITISH RAIL
REGRETS THE
DELAY OF THE
8·28 FROM COLCHESTER
THIS WAS DUE TO
LEAVES
LINE
ENGINEERING WORKS
LOST THE MAP
ATTACKED BY ALIEN SPACE CRAFT

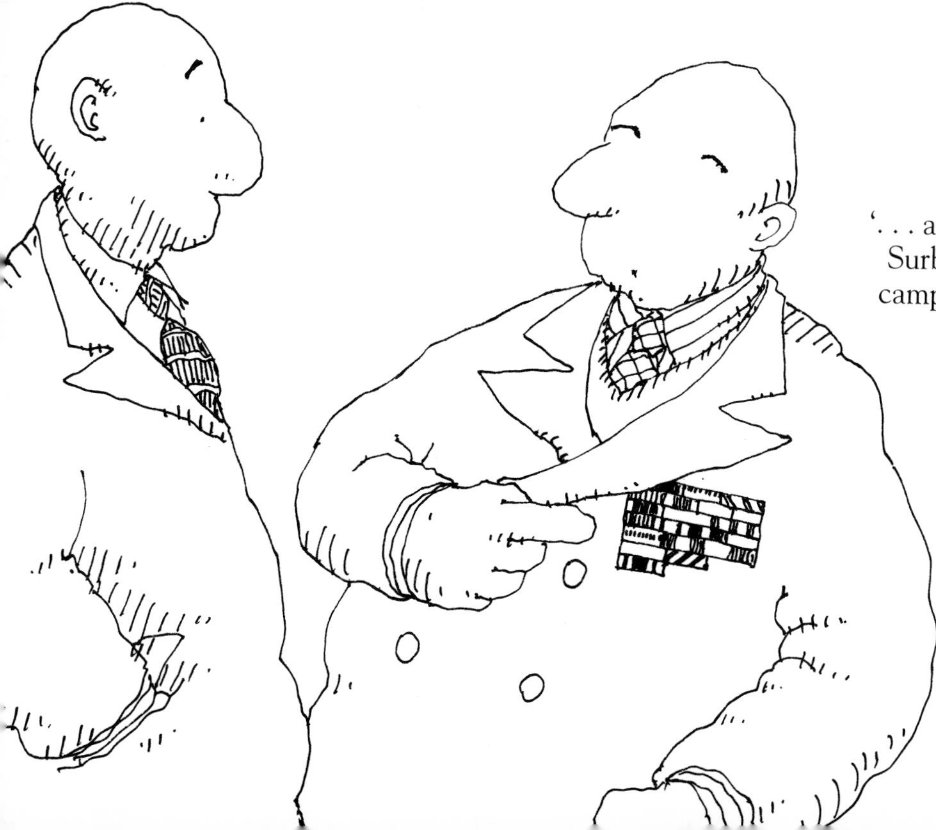

'. . . and this is for the Surbiton Waterloo campaign of '63 . . .'

# THE AWAY DAY

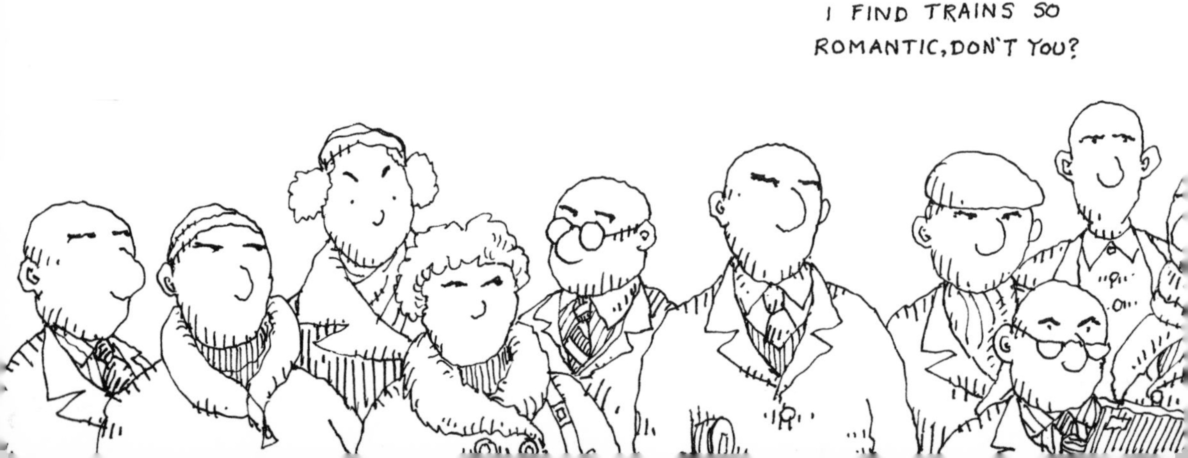
I FIND TRAINS SO ROMANTIC, DON'T YOU?

# Classic Commuter Cartoons. Number 1

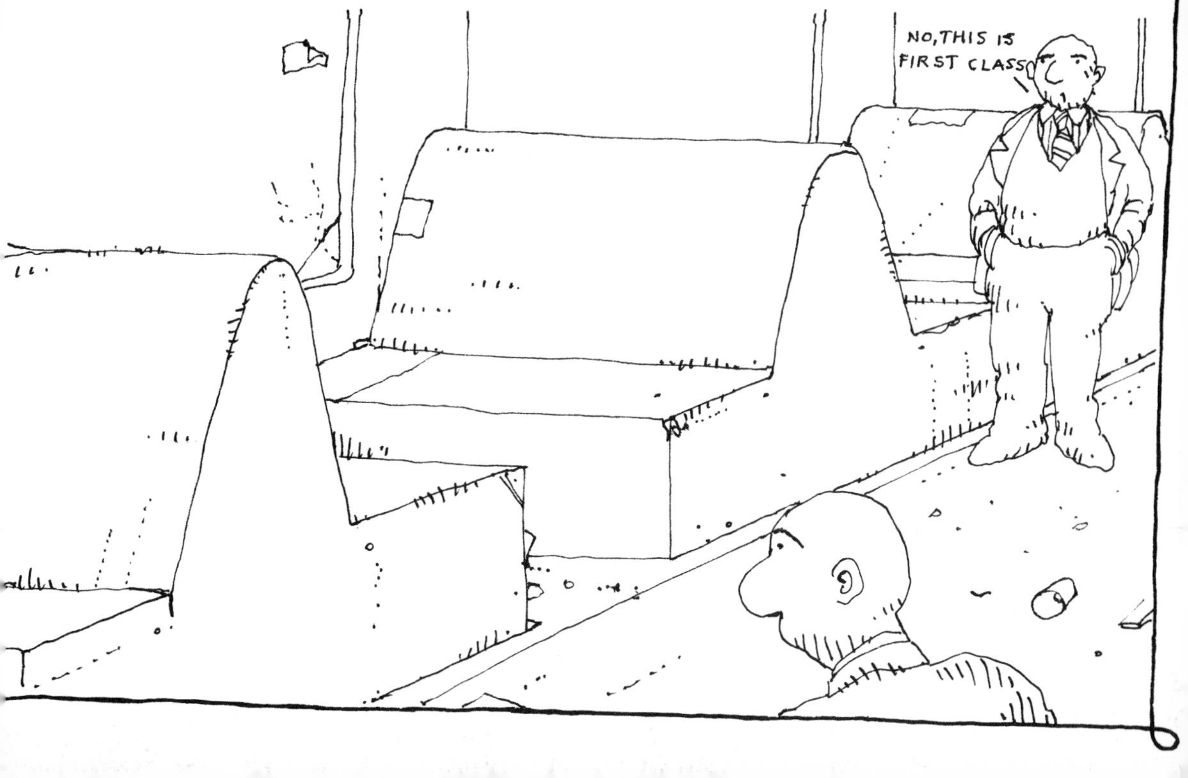

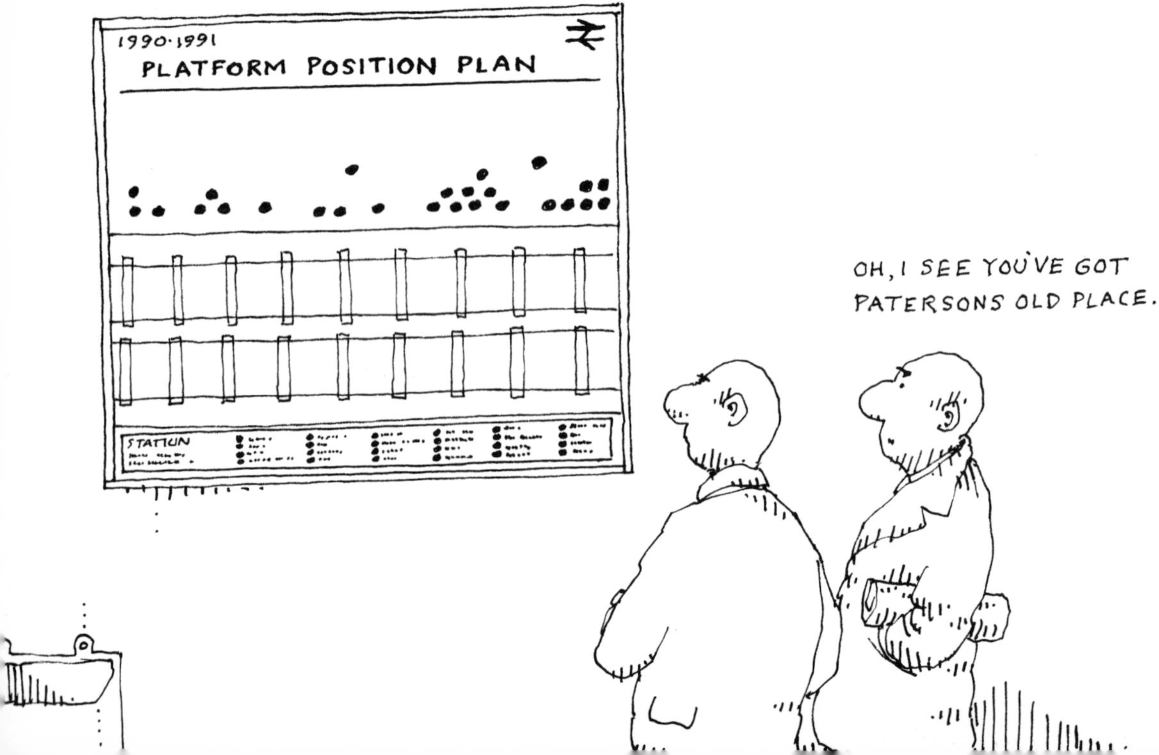
1990·1991
PLATFORM POSITION PLAN
STATION

OH, I SEE YOU'VE GOT PATERSONS OLD PLACE.

CONSOLATION

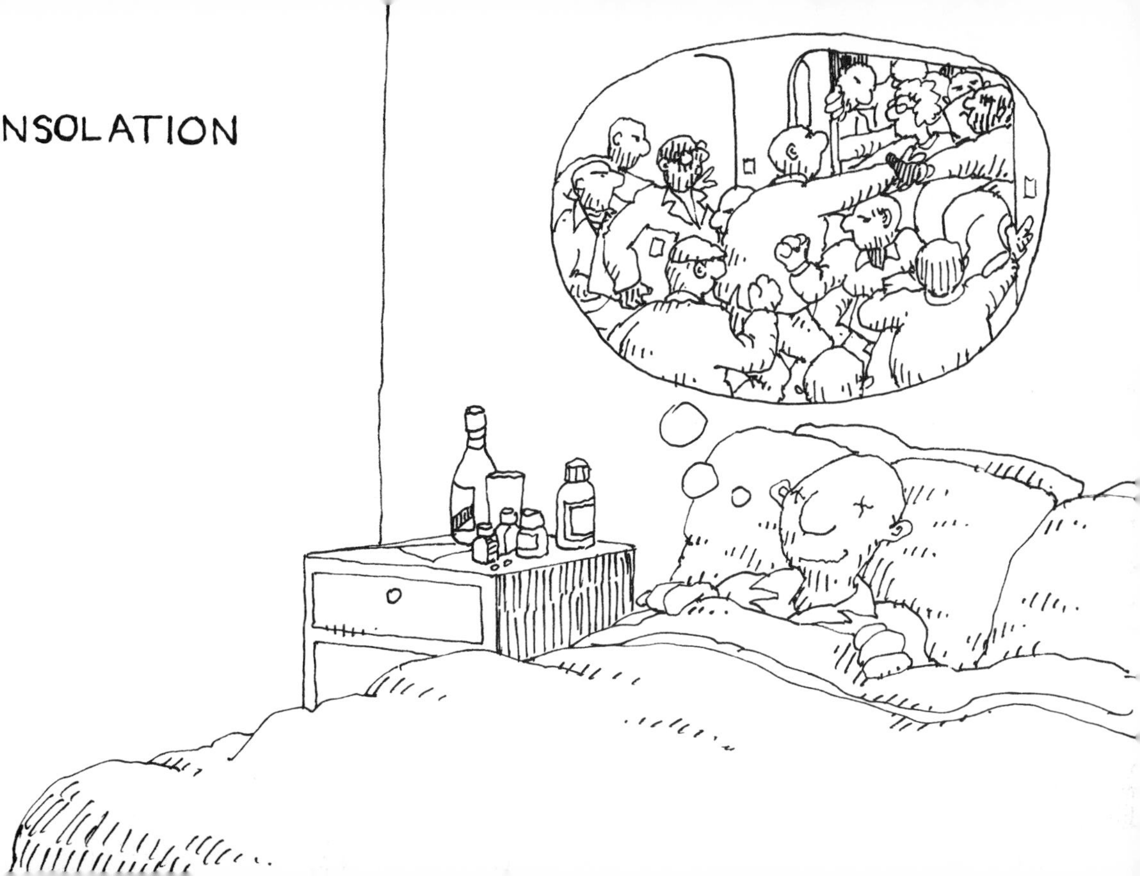

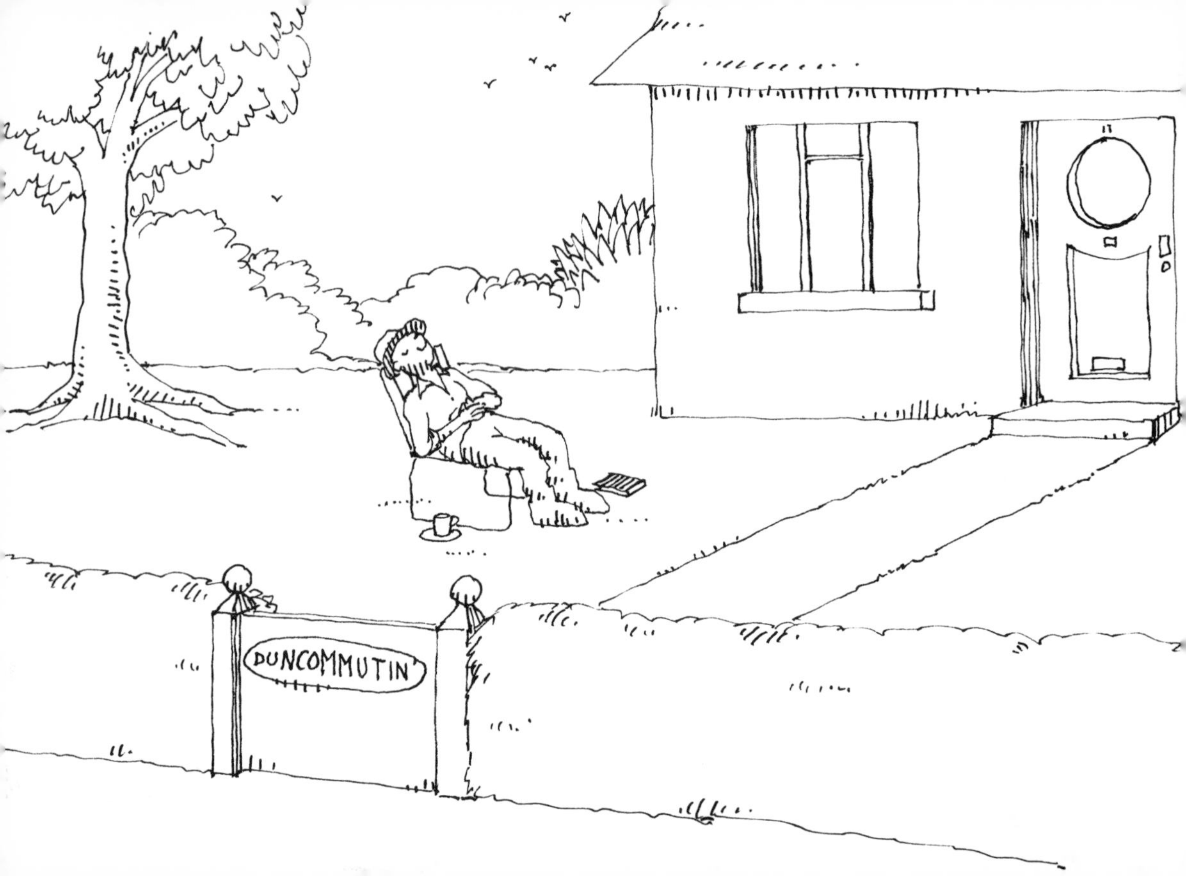
DUNCOMMUTIN'

B.R. ORGANIZES DUNKIRK

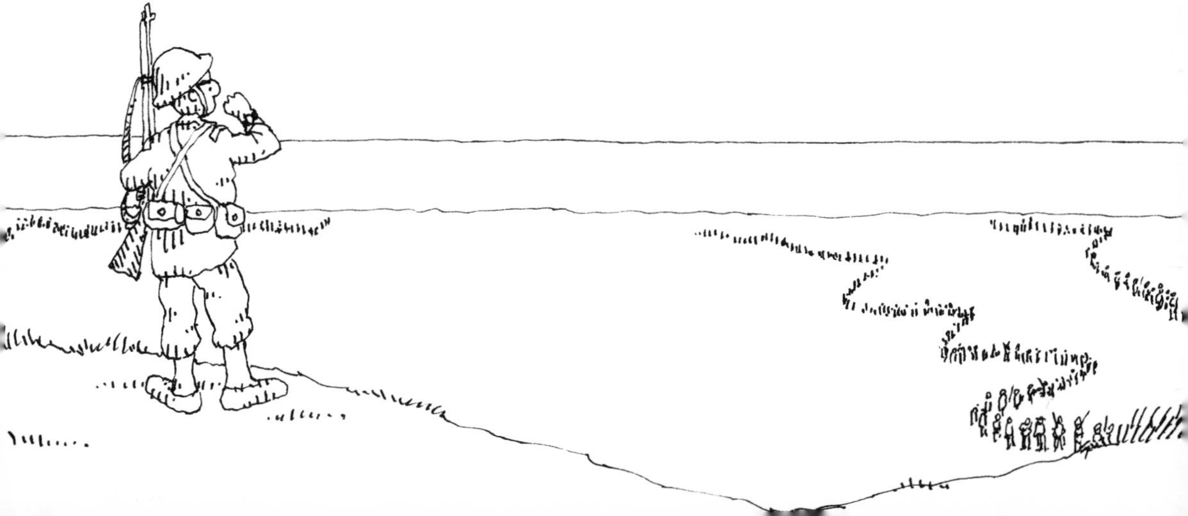

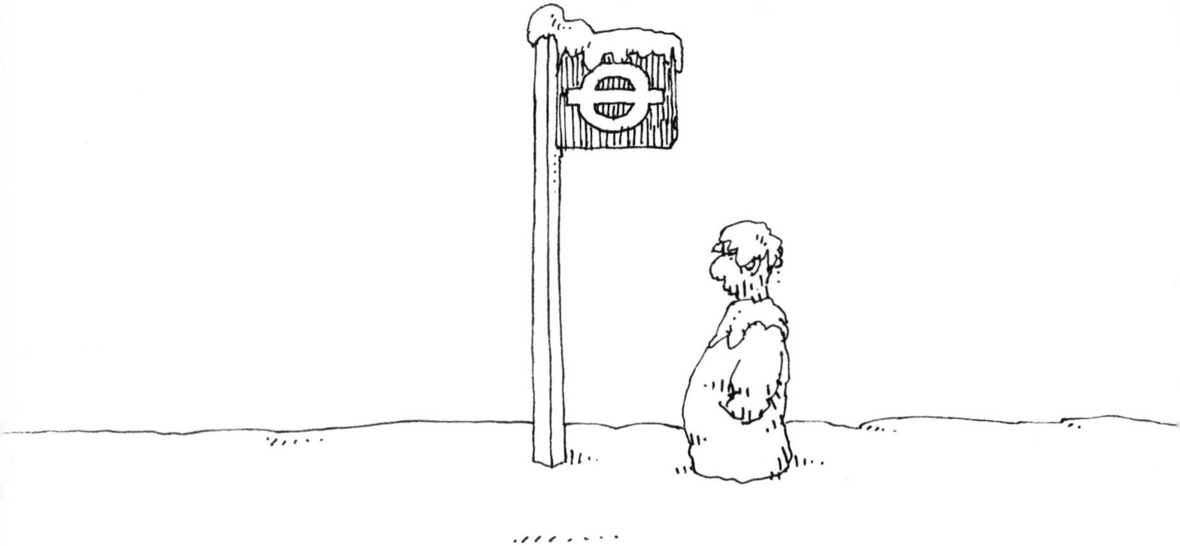

The Optimist

The 6.06 to Brighton overshoots the buffers.

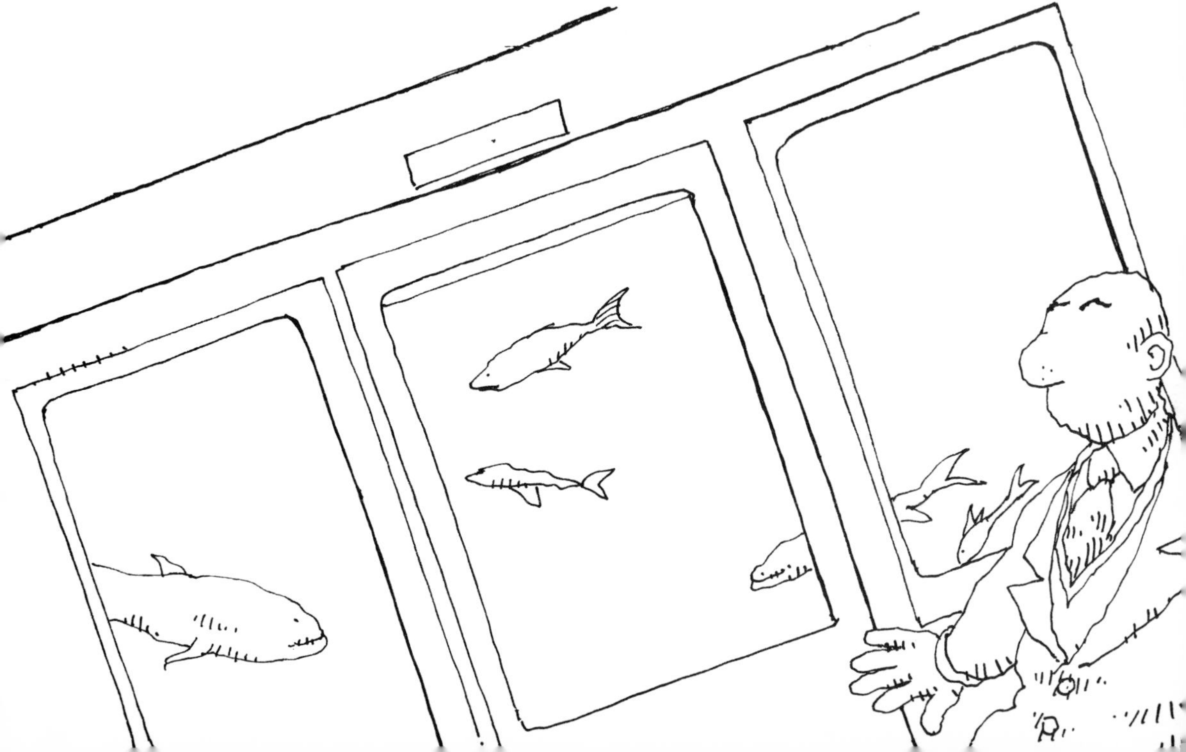

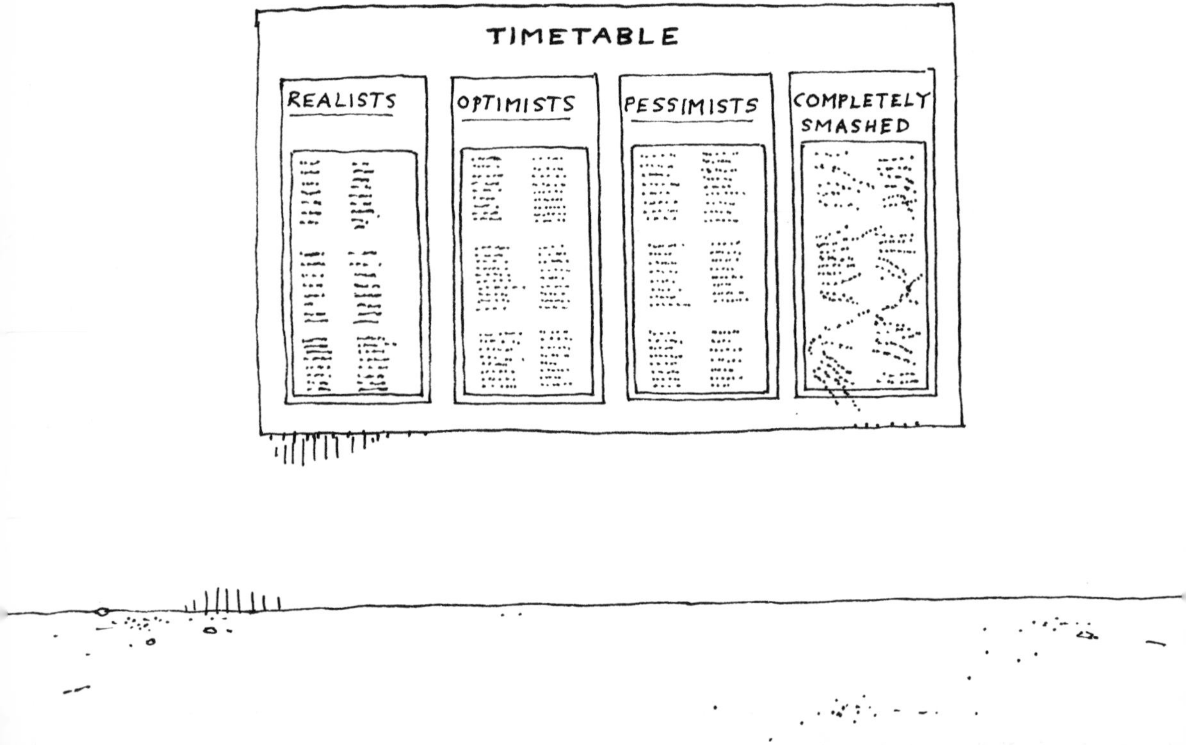
TIMETABLE
REALISTS
OPTIMISTS
PESSIMISTS
COMPLETELY SMASHED

# QUESTIONAIRE

* PLEASE TICK THE APPROPRIATE BOX

| REASONS FOR COMMUTING | |
|---|---|
| WORK | |
| PLEASURE | |
| SADO-MASOCHISTIC TENDENCIES | |
| SEVERE CHARACTER FLAW | |
| HOBBY/SPORT | |
| OTHER | |

| WAYS TO IMPROVE THE SERVICES | |
|---|---|
| MORE FUNDING | |
| EXTRA STAFF | |
| IMPROVE CATERING | |
| BAN POLYSTYRENE CUPS | |
| FIRE-BOMB ALL MAINLINE STATIONS | |
| THEN PAINT ALL THE RAILS YELLOW AND CALL IN DOROTHY | |

LEONARD VOSSMAN & HIS HIGH OCTANE SOCKS

# HOLMES CONFIRMS THE RUMOUR.

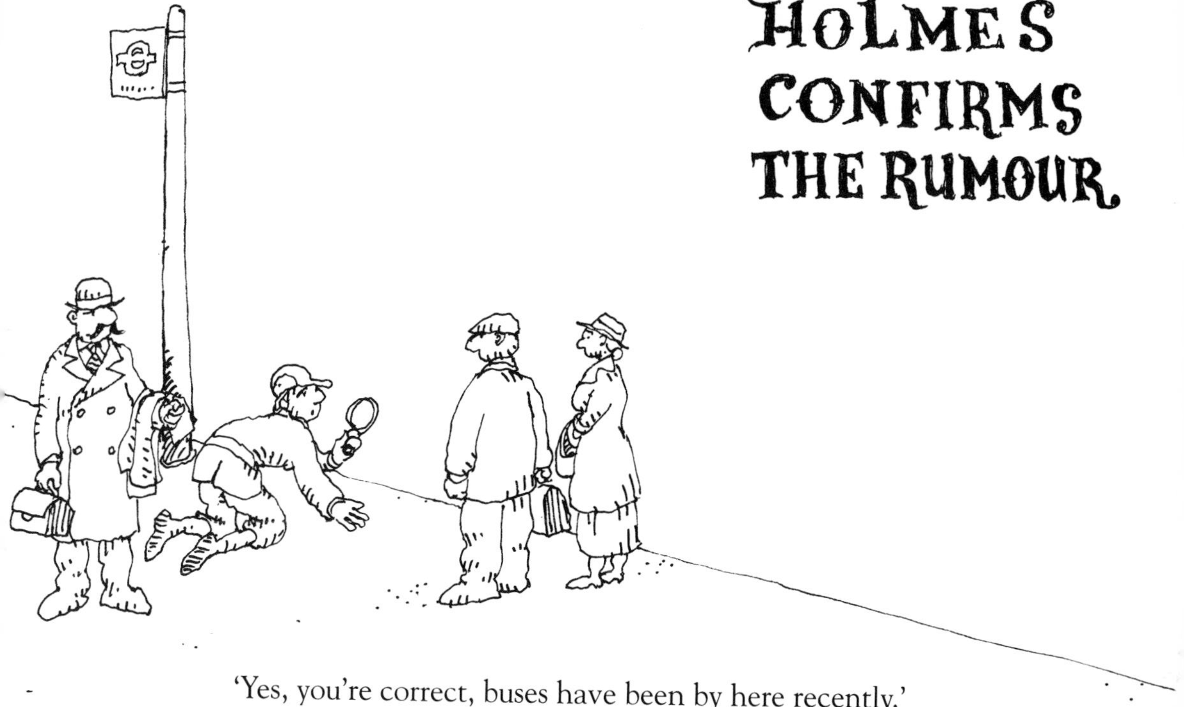

'Yes, you're correct, buses have been by here recently.'

THE BRITISH RAIL S.E. REGIONS GLEE CLUB BURSTS INTO LIFE

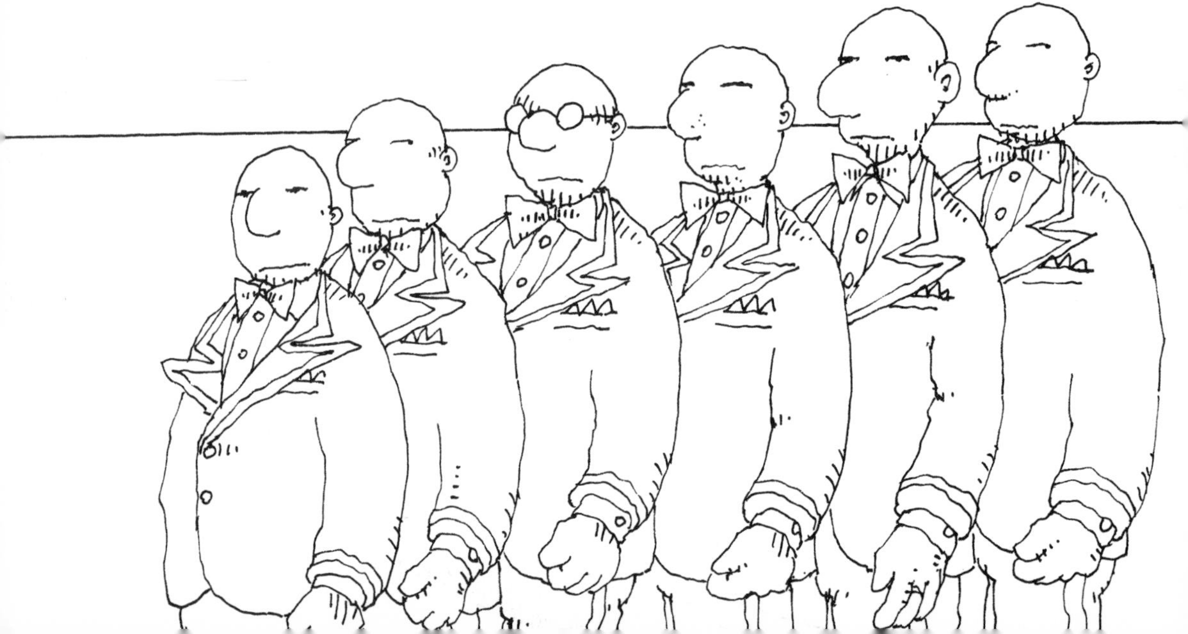

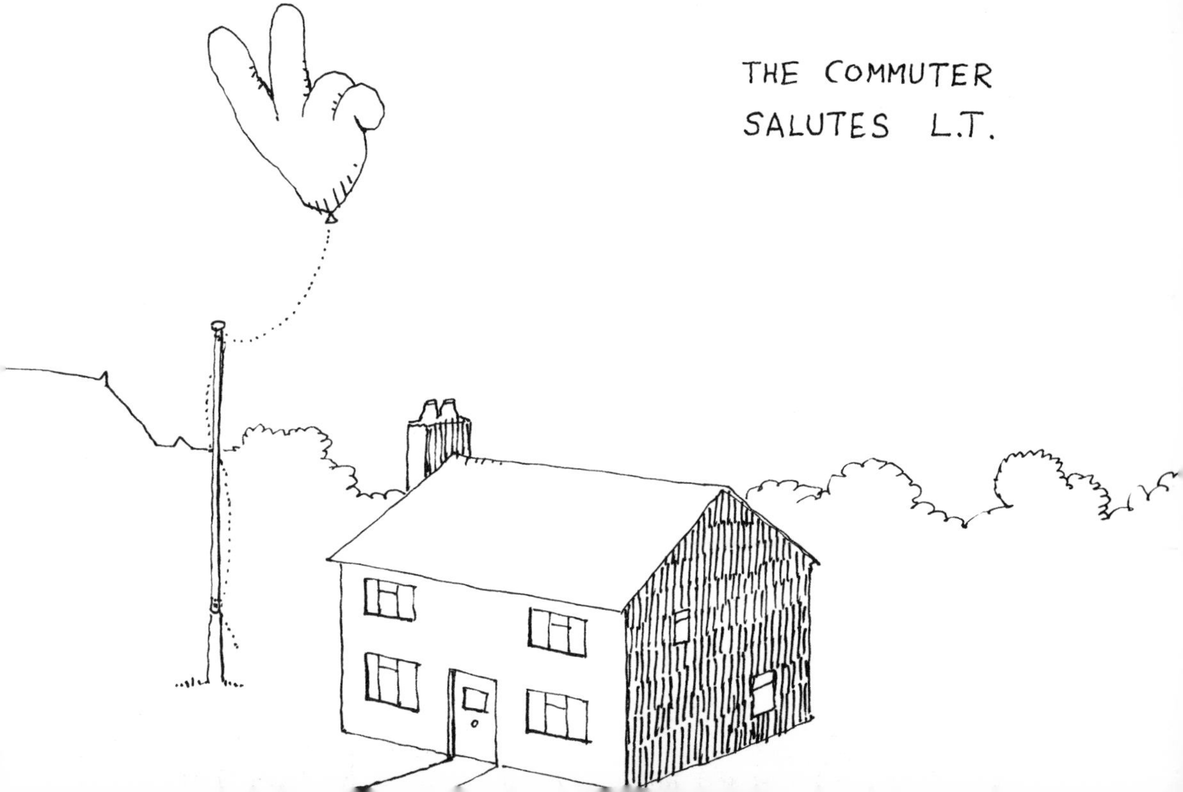

THE COMMUTER SALUTES L.T.

'You are going on a long journey . . . with two breakdowns and no restaurant facilities . . .'

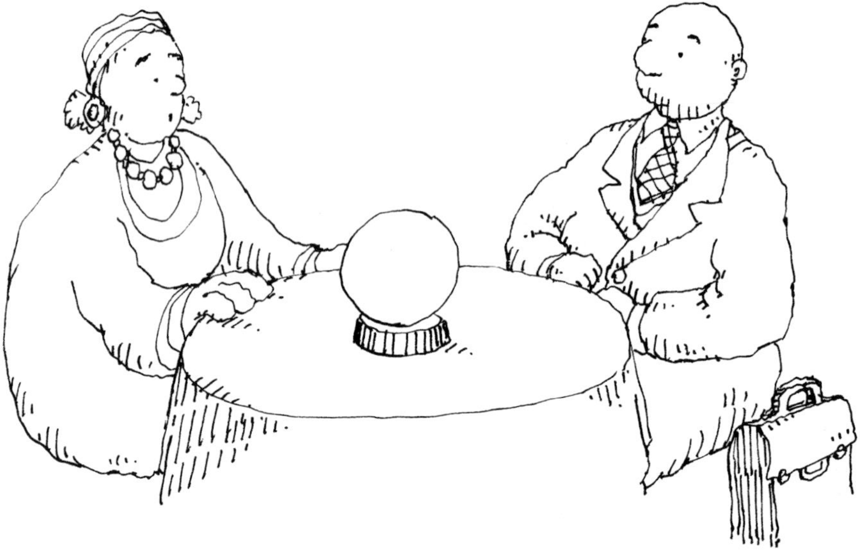

OKAY, PUNK, MAKE MY DAY.

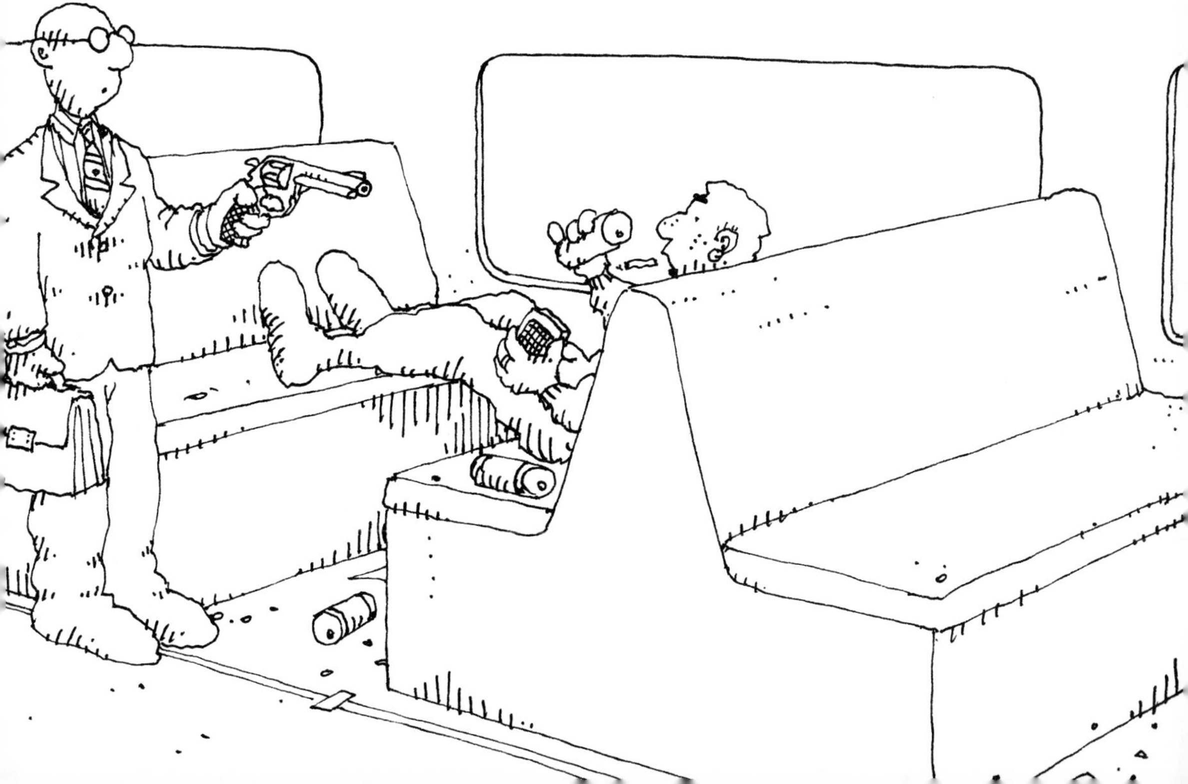

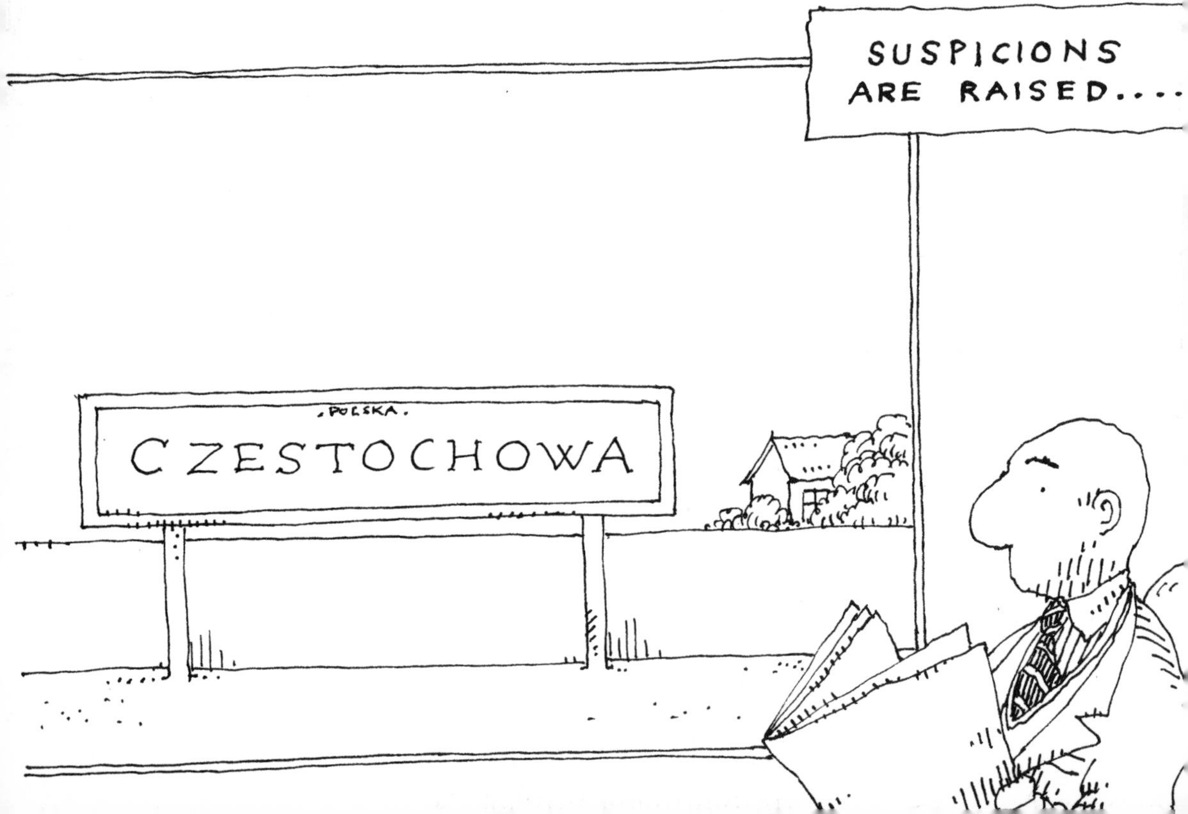
SUSPICIONS
ARE RAISED....
POLSKA
CZESTOCHOWA

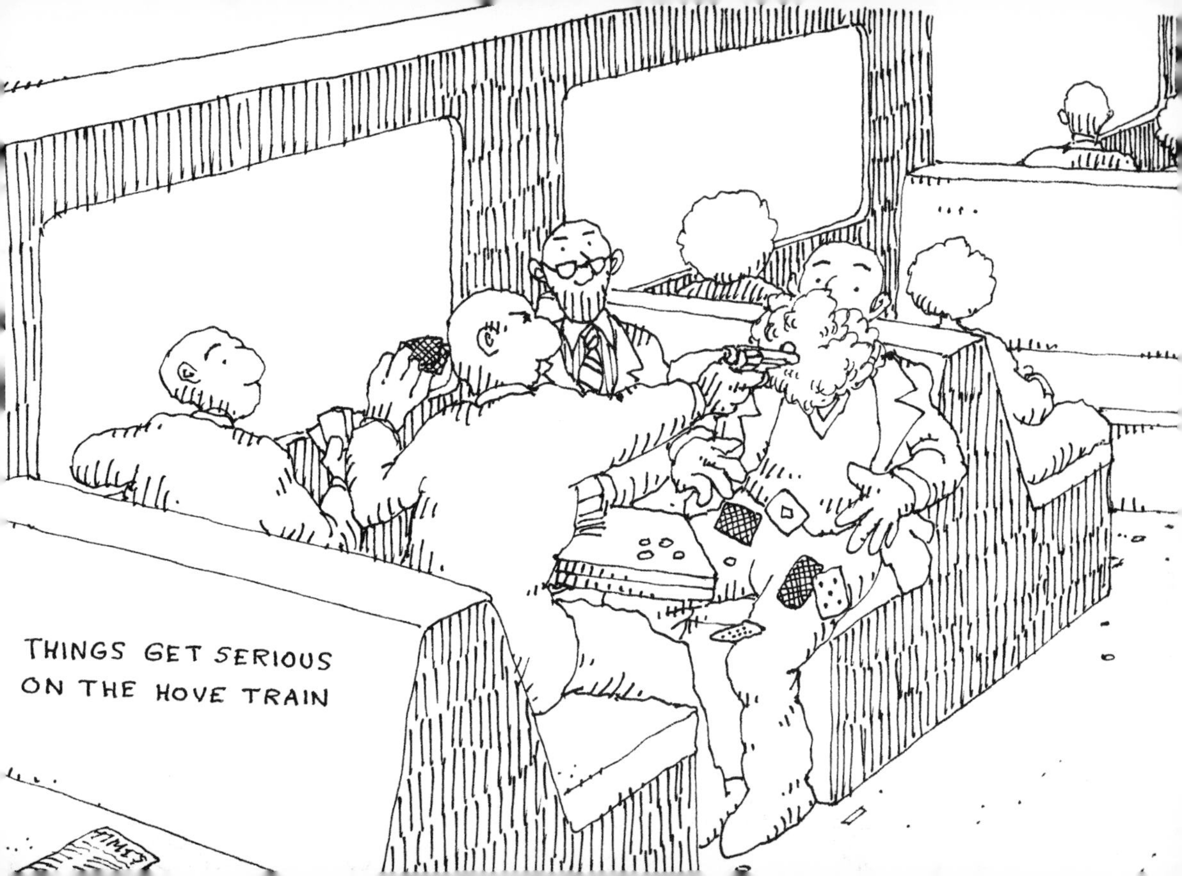
THINGS GET SERIOUS
ON THE HOVE TRAIN
TIMES

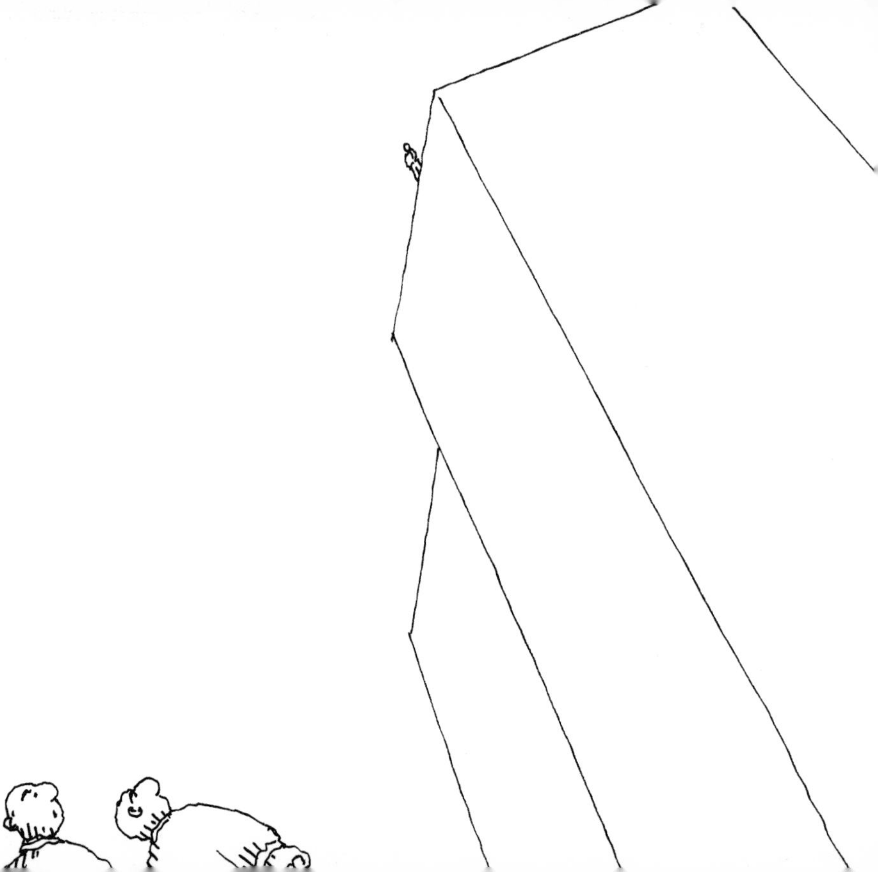

He lost his
season ticket.

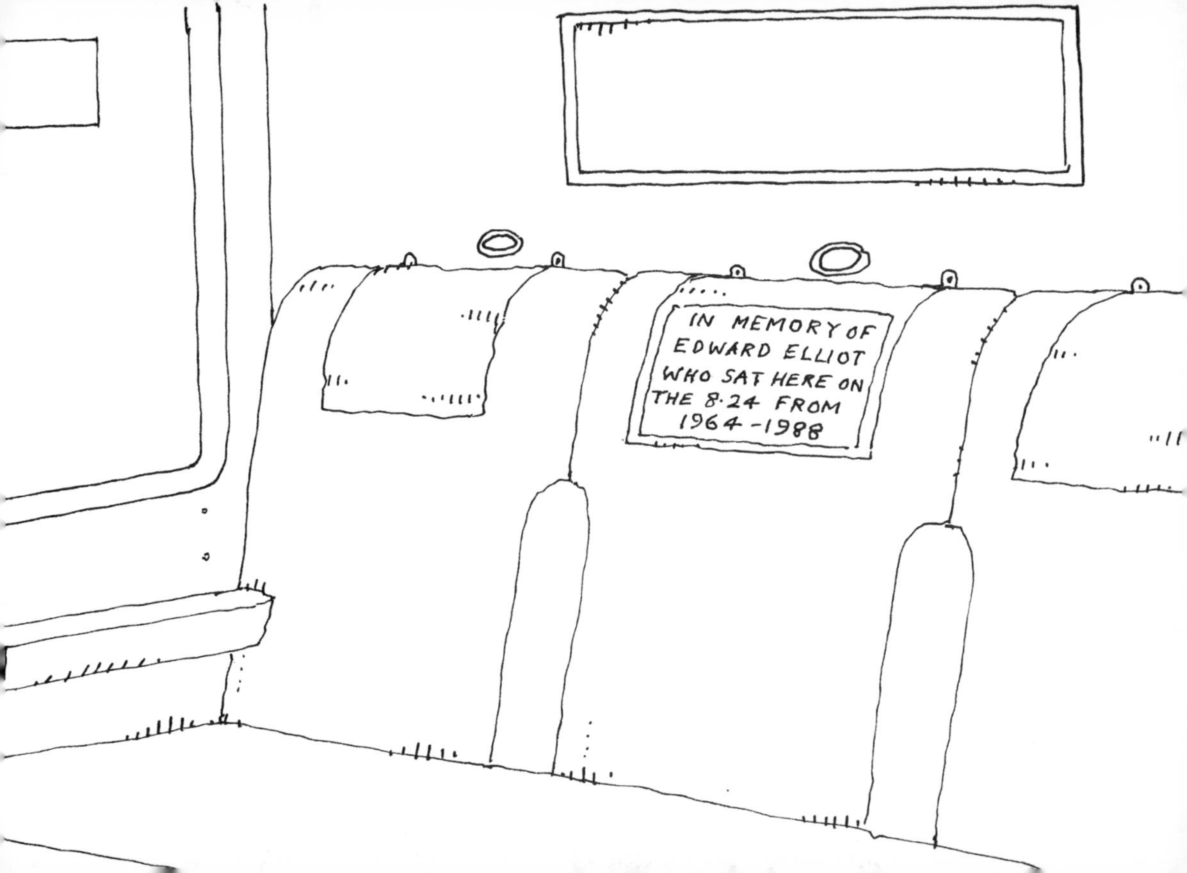
IN MEMORY OF
EDWARD ELLIOT
WHO SAT HERE ON
THE 8·24 FROM
1964 -1988

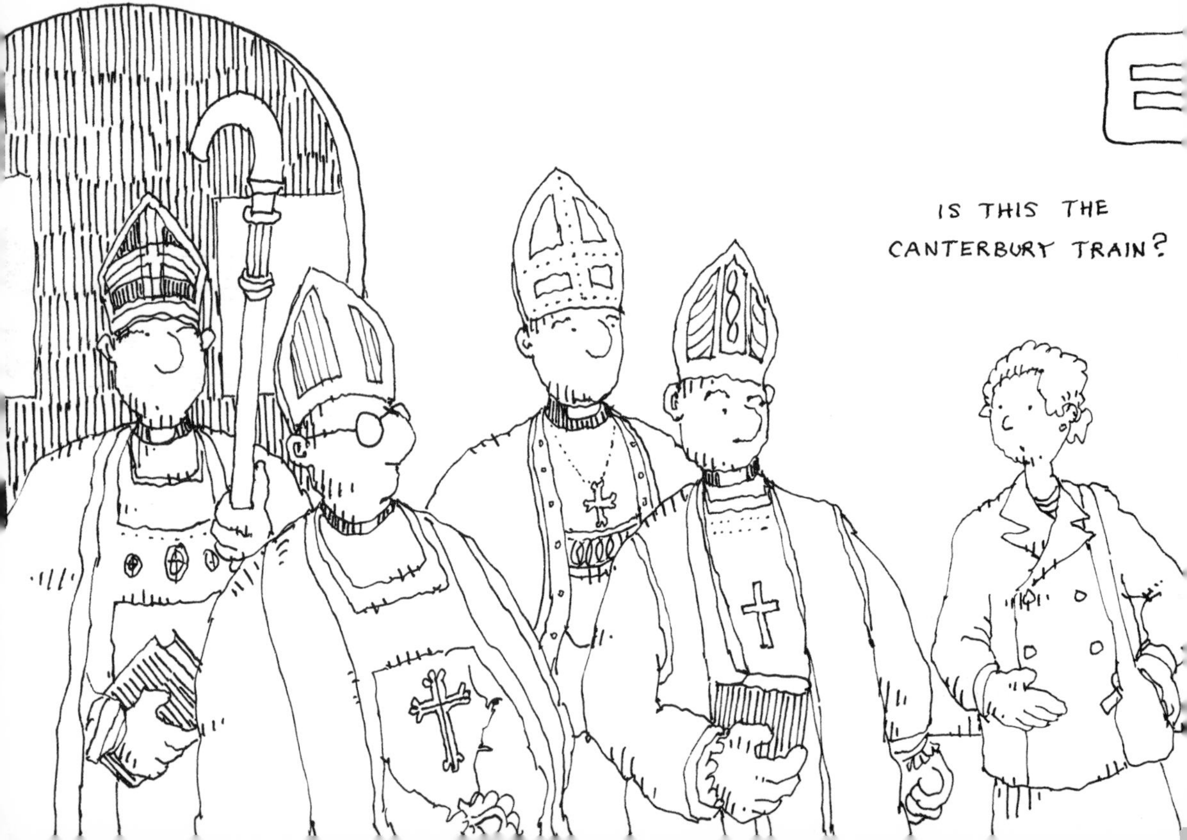
IS THIS THE CANTERBURY TRAIN?

TEMPERS FRAY
AFTER A DELAY
AT LITTLE DABNEY HALT

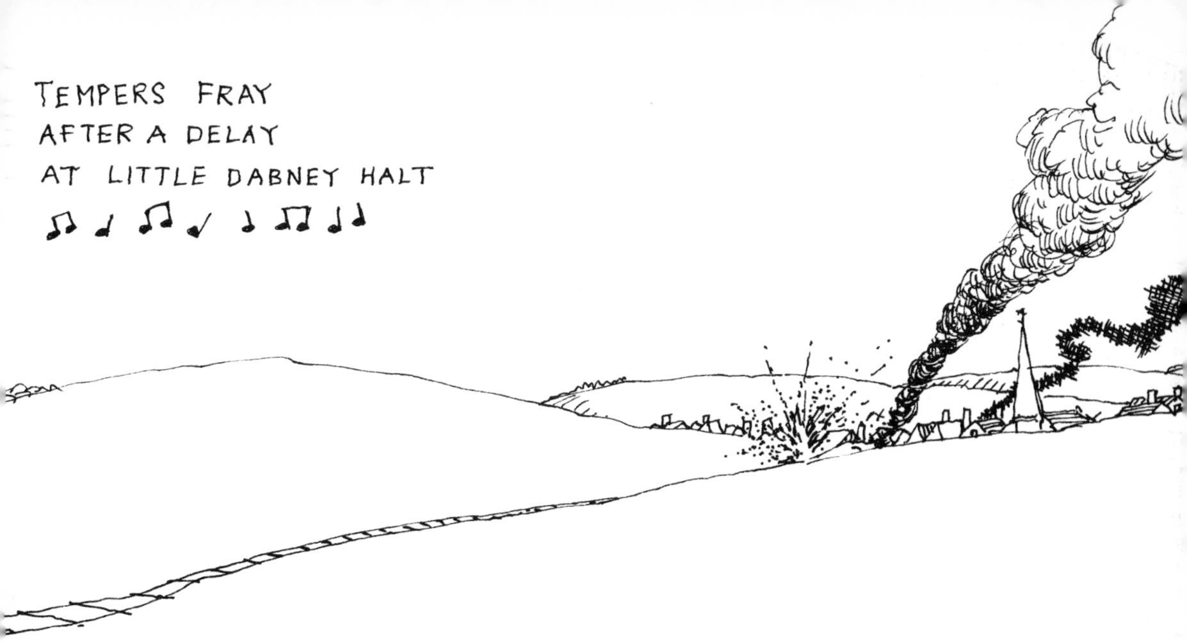

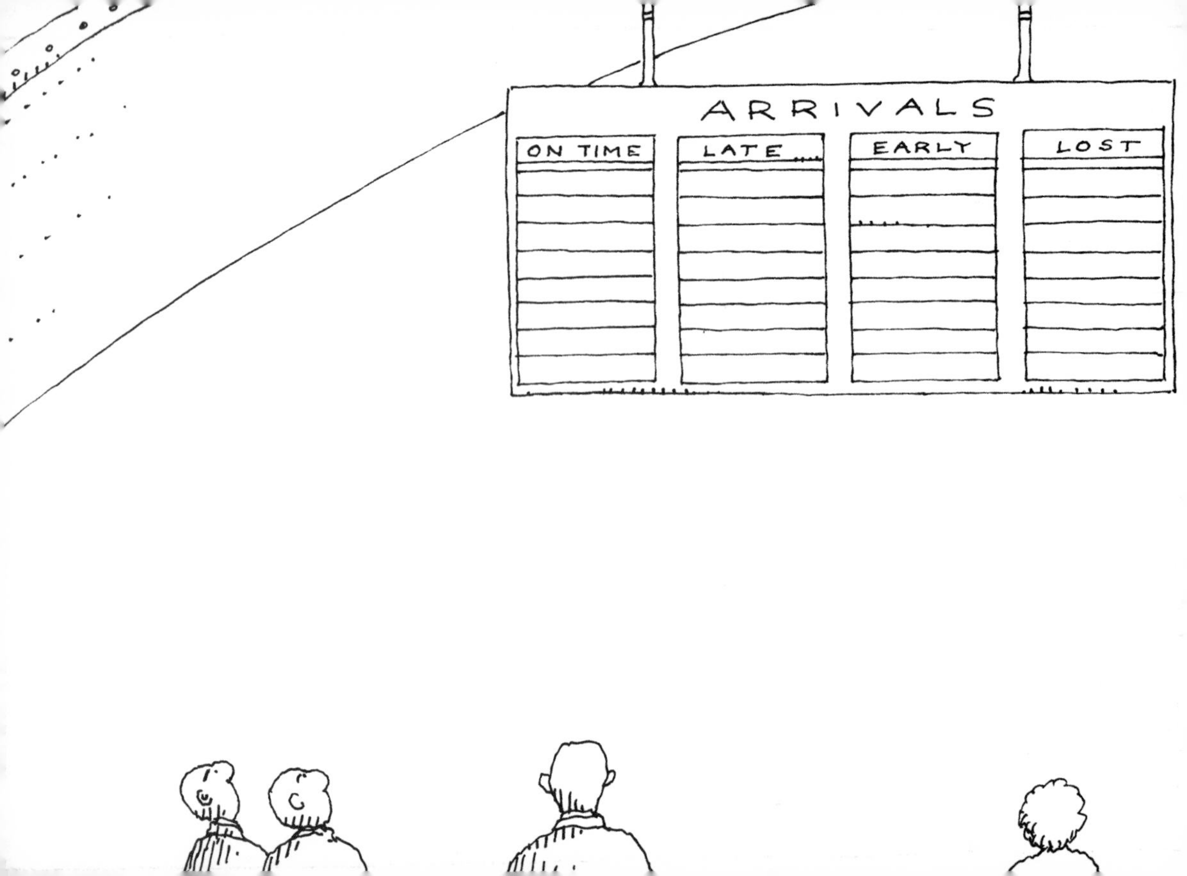
ARRIVALS
ON TIME
LATE
EARLY
LOST

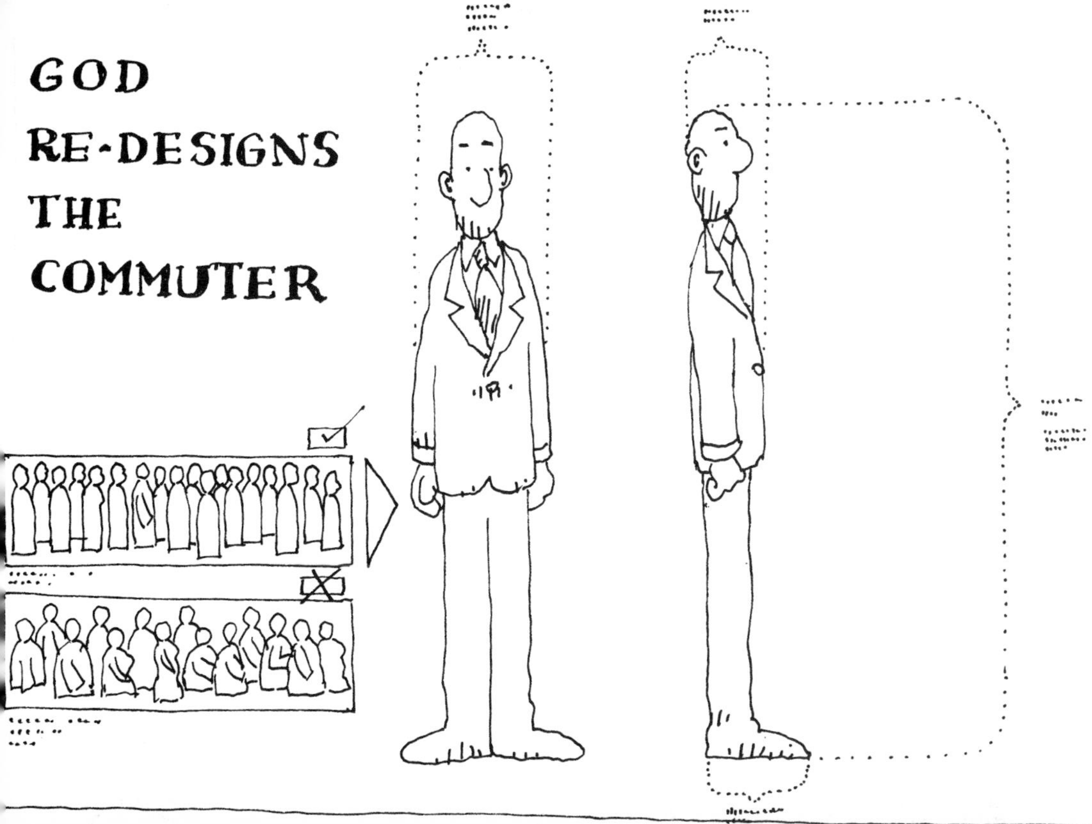
GOD
RE-DESIGNS
THE
COMMUTER

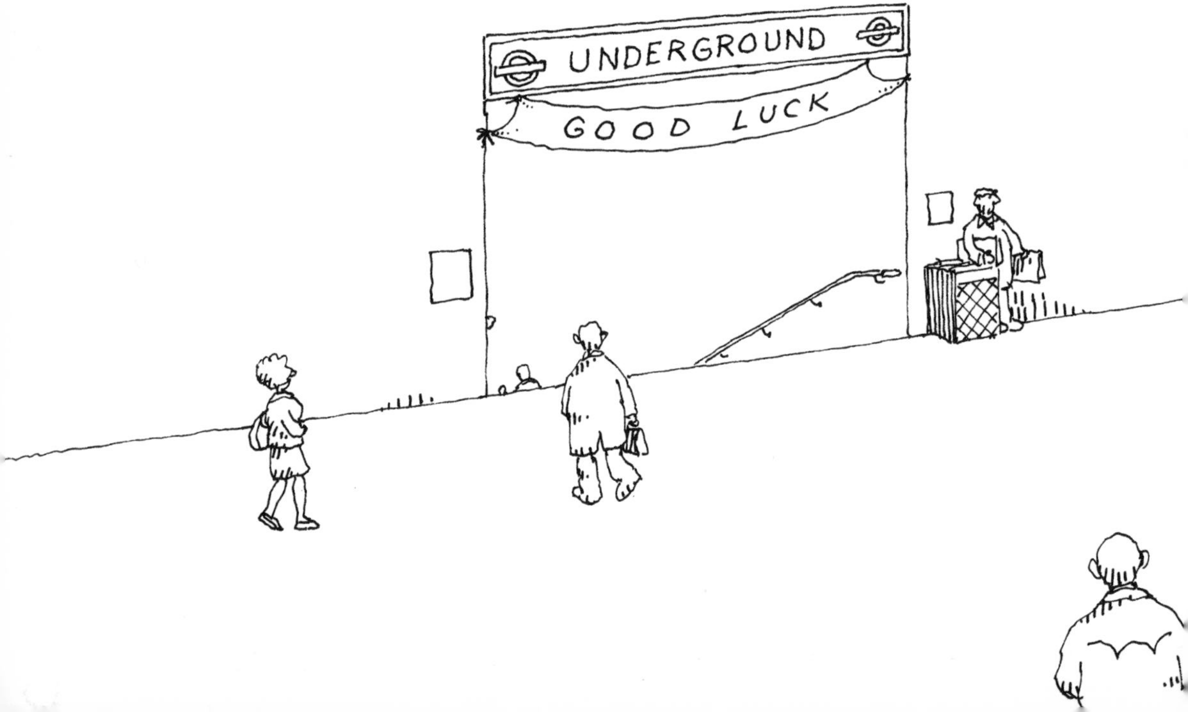
UNDERGROUND
GOOD LUCK

# Classic Commuter Cartoons. Number 2

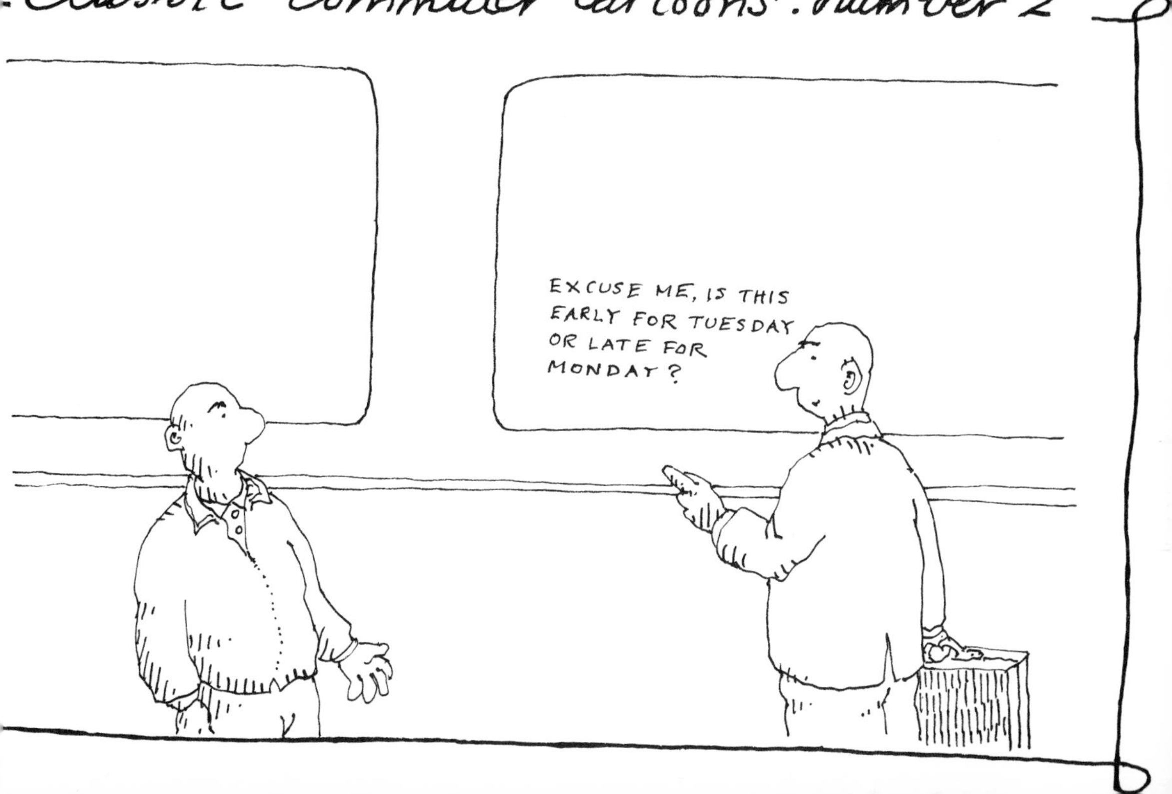

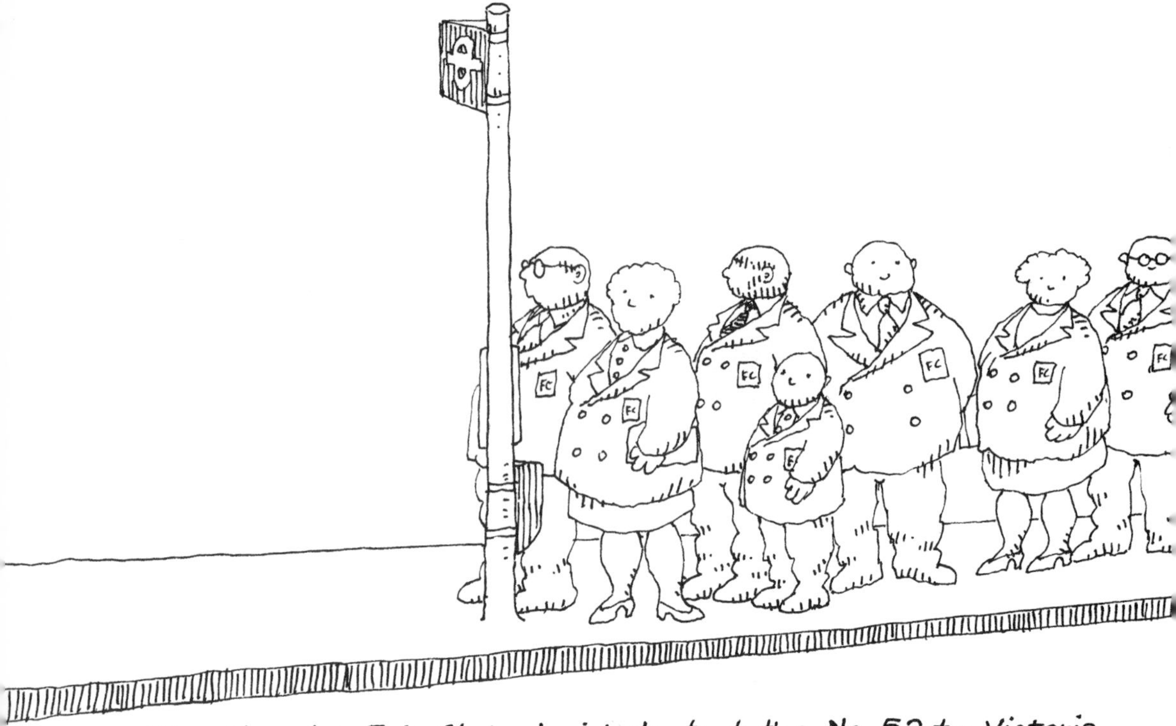
FC

The Neasden Fat Club decide to test the No. 52 to Victoria.

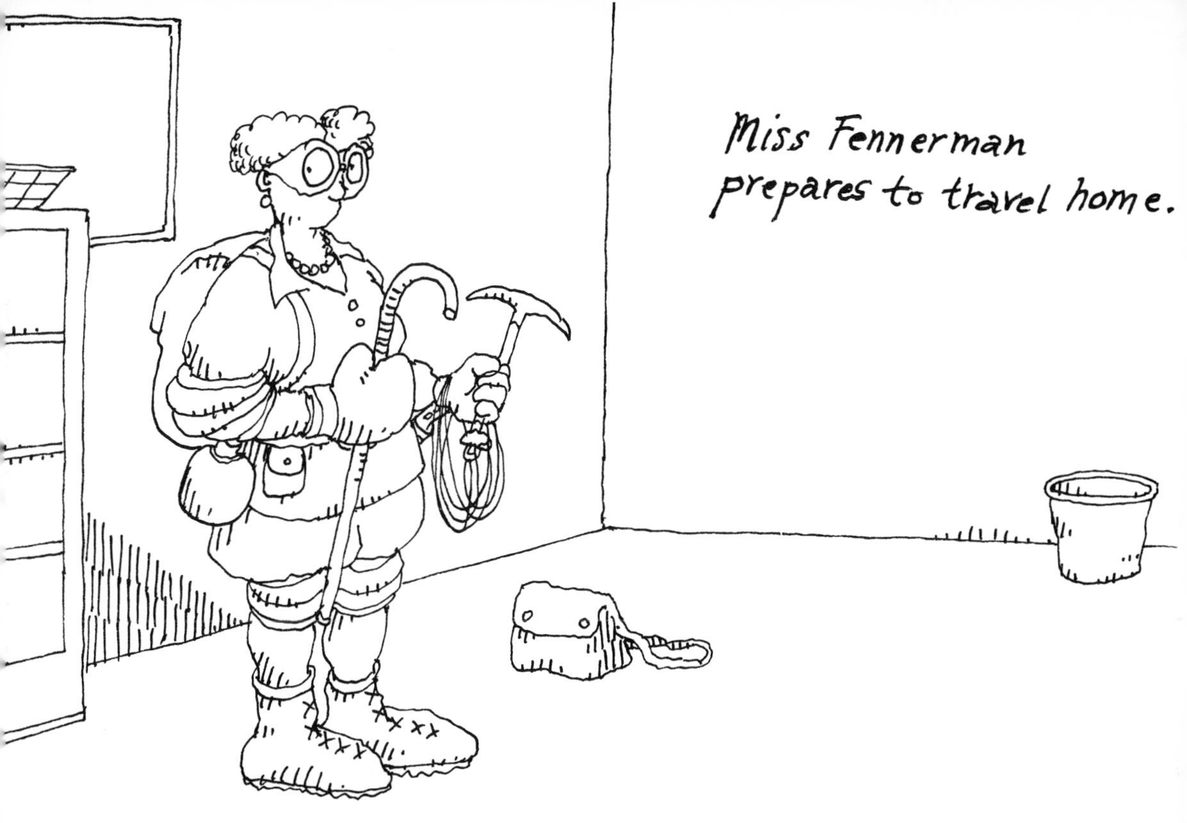

Miss Fennerman prepares to travel home.

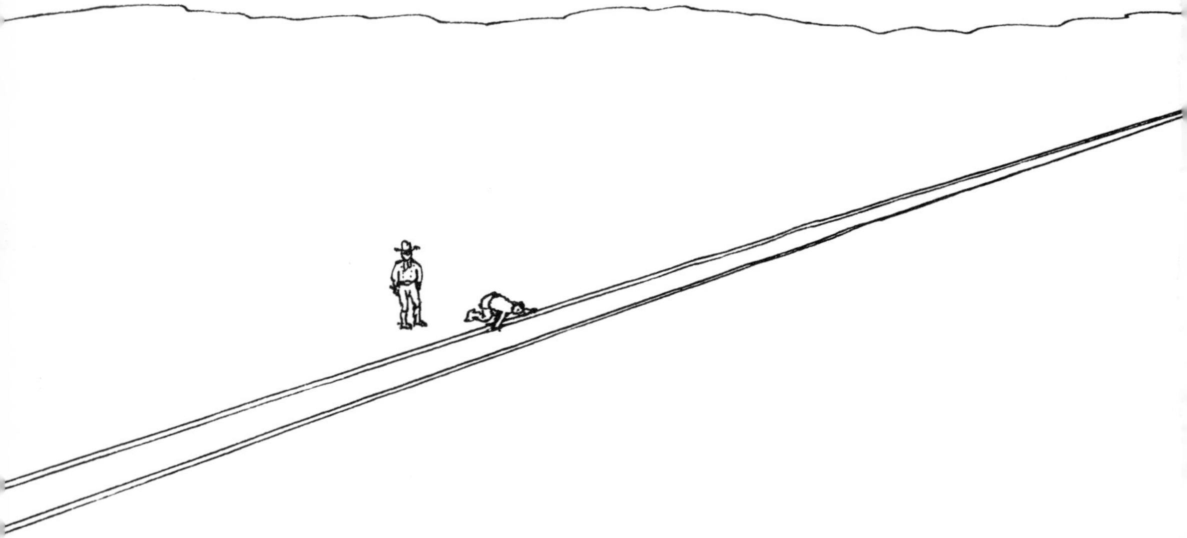

'Relax Kemo Sabi . . . the Worthing train is on time.'

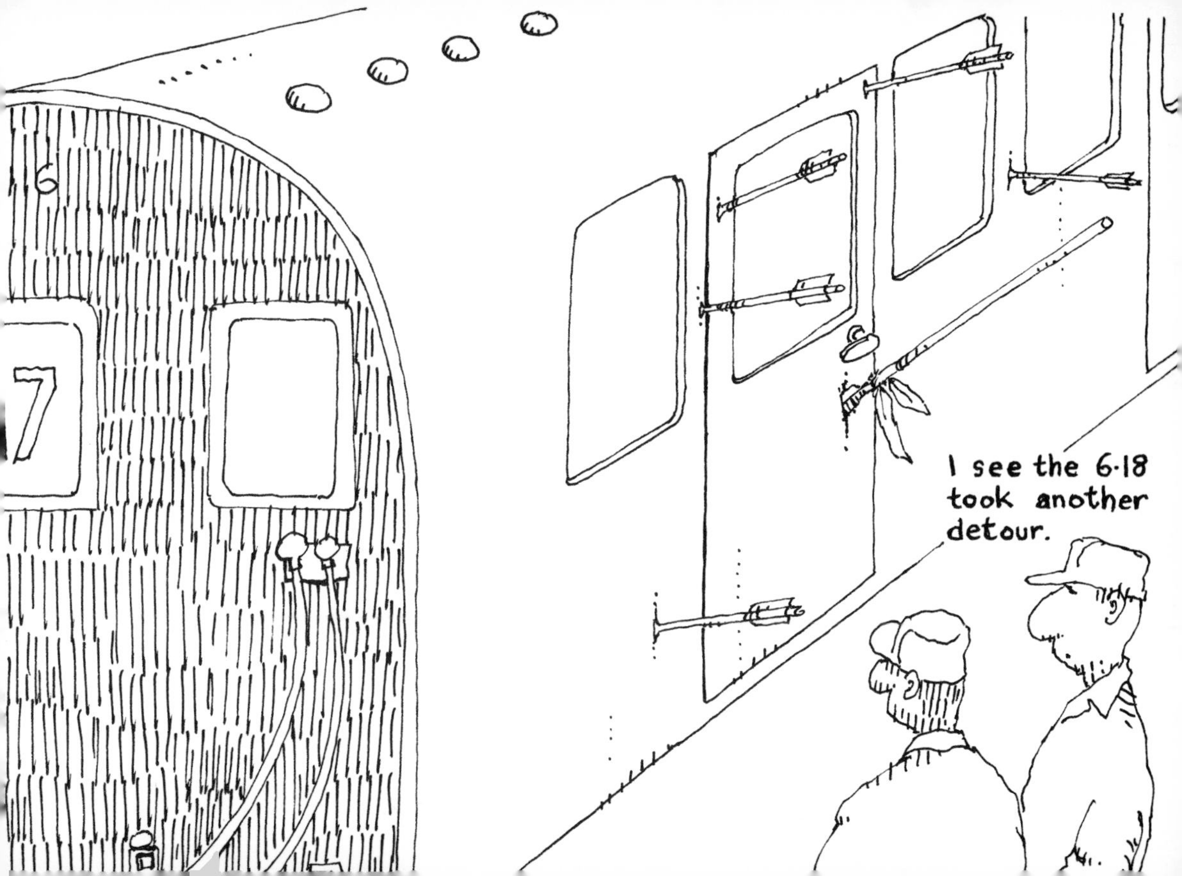
I see the 6·18 took another detour.

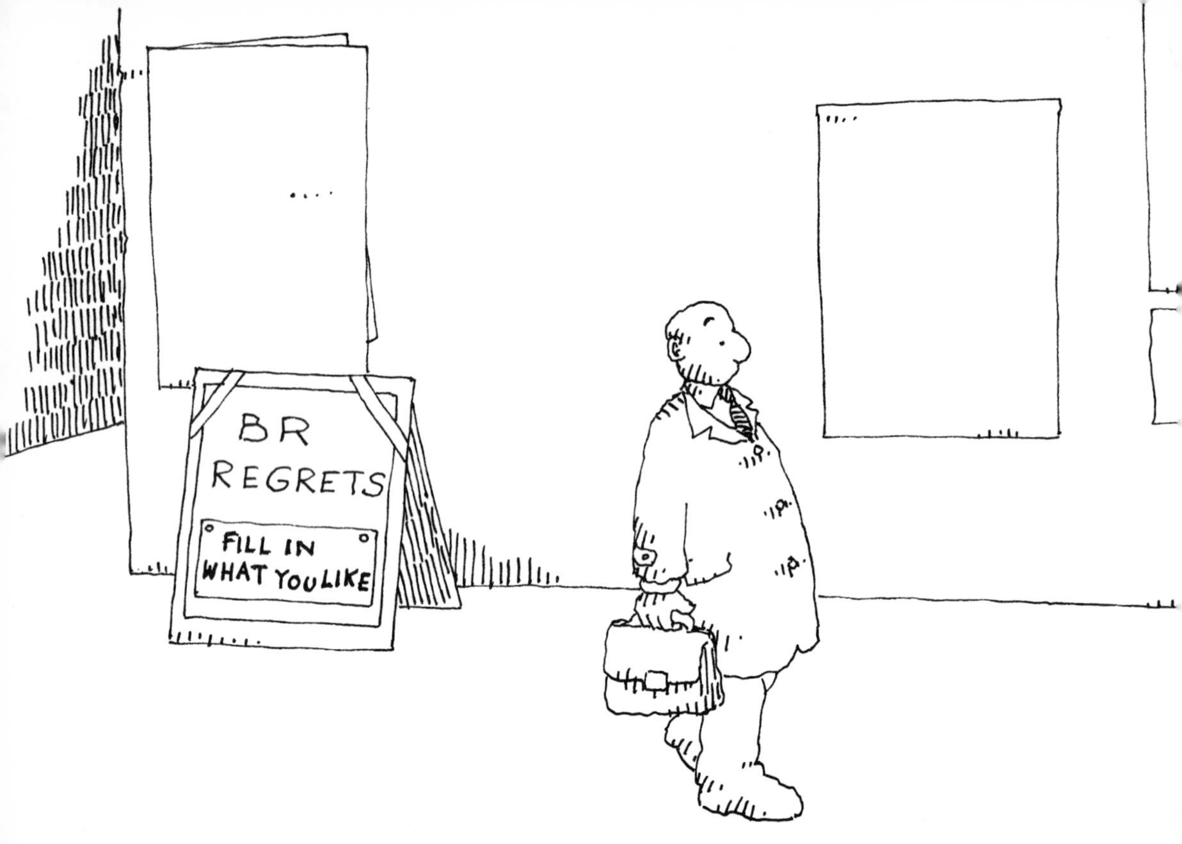
BR
REGRETS
FILL IN
WHAT YOU LIKE

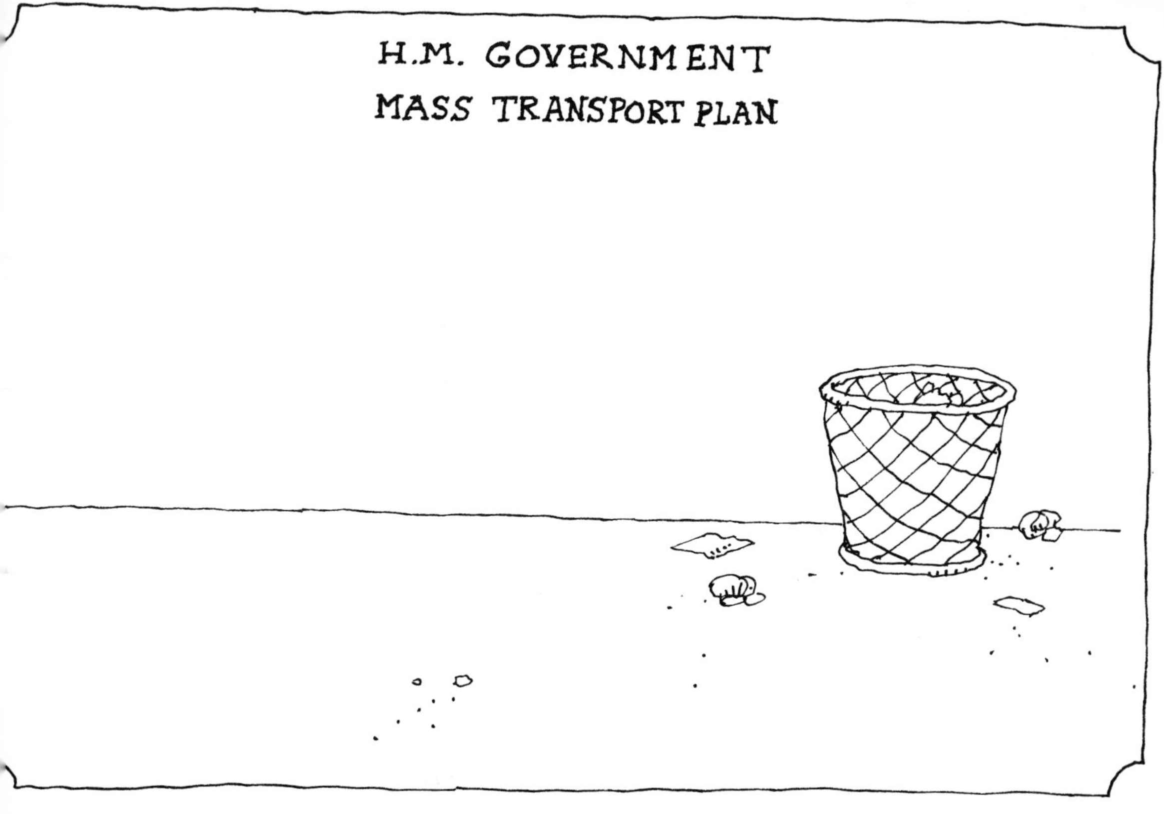
H.M. GOVERNMENT
MASS TRANSPORT PLAN

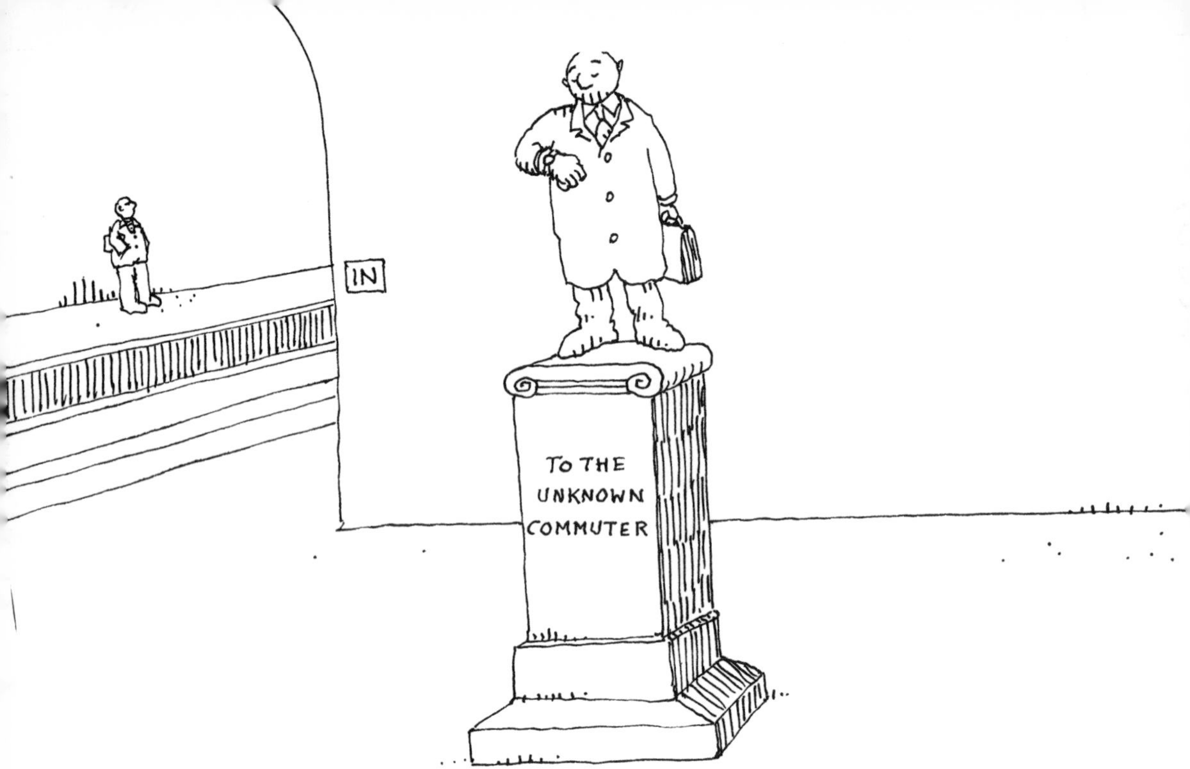
IN
TO THE
UNKNOWN
COMMUTER

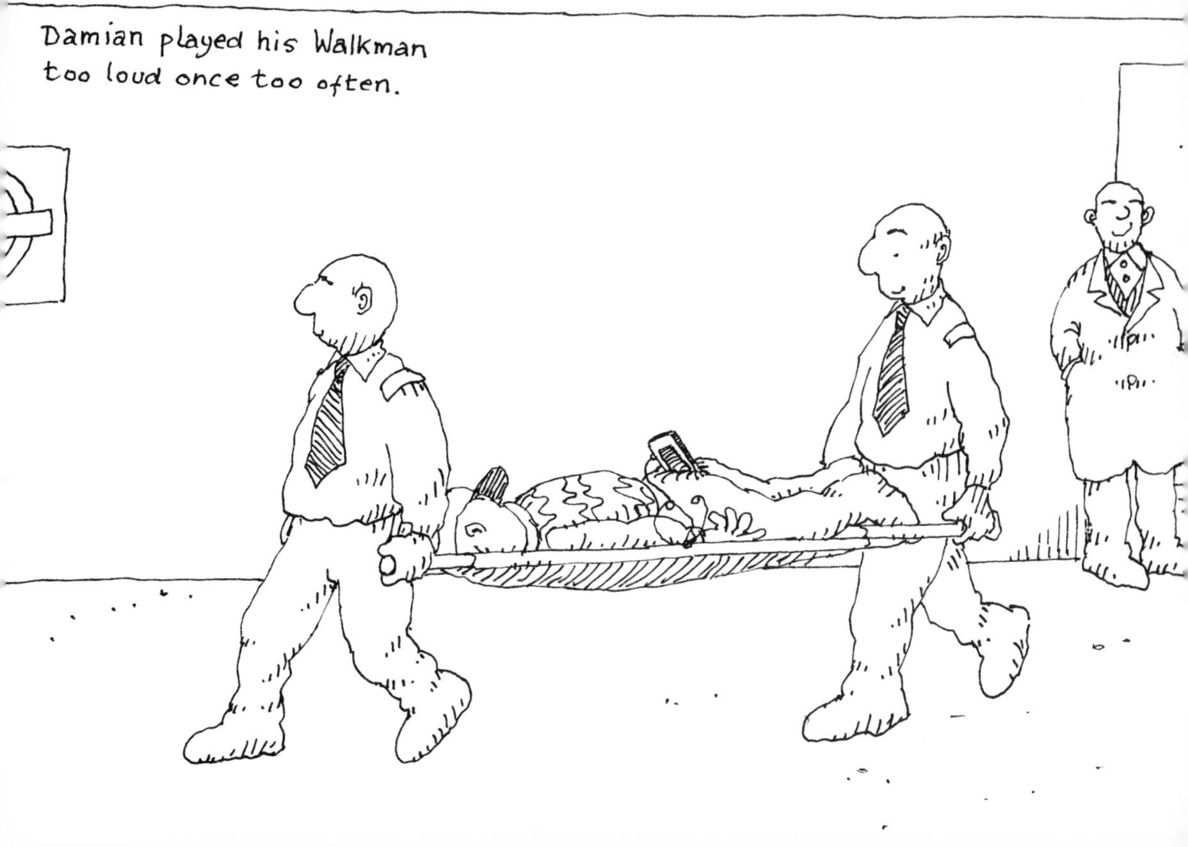
Damian played his Walkman too loud once too often.

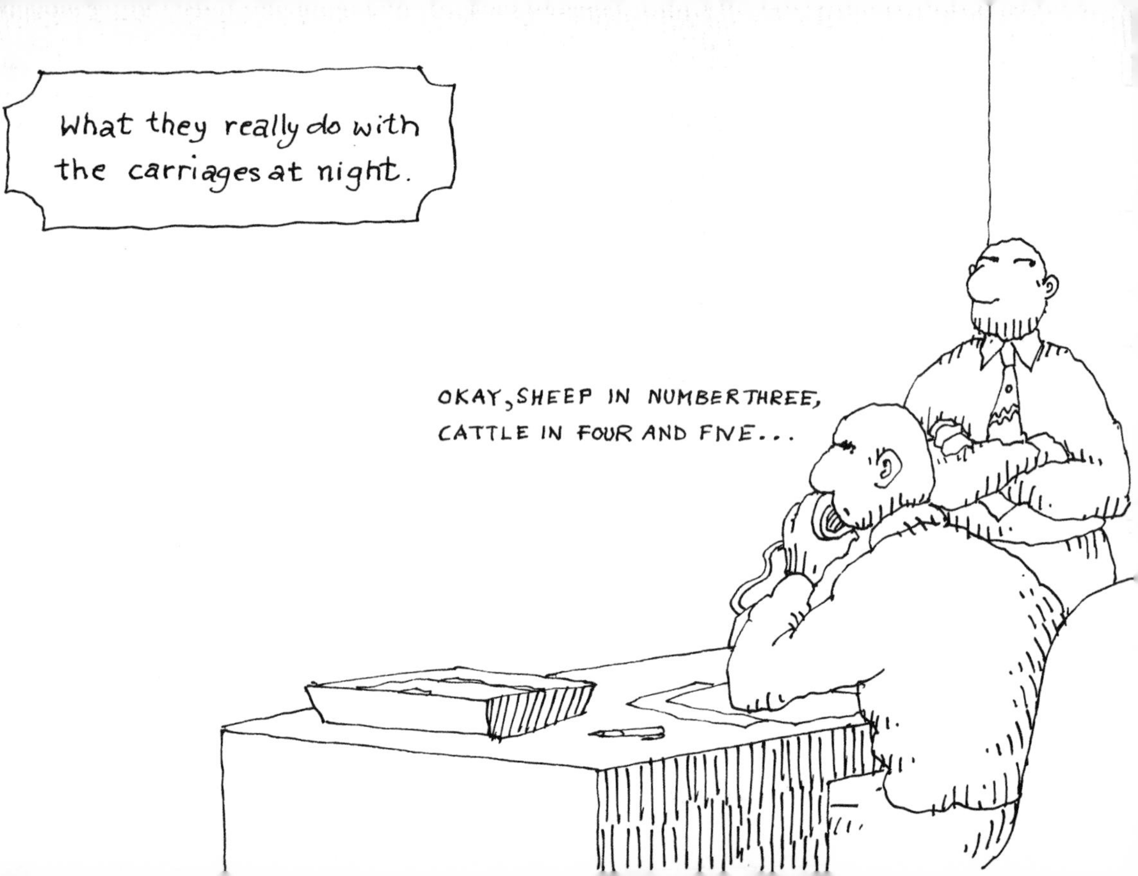
What they really do with the carriages at night.
OKAY, SHEEP IN NUMBER THREE, CATTLE IN FOUR AND FIVE...

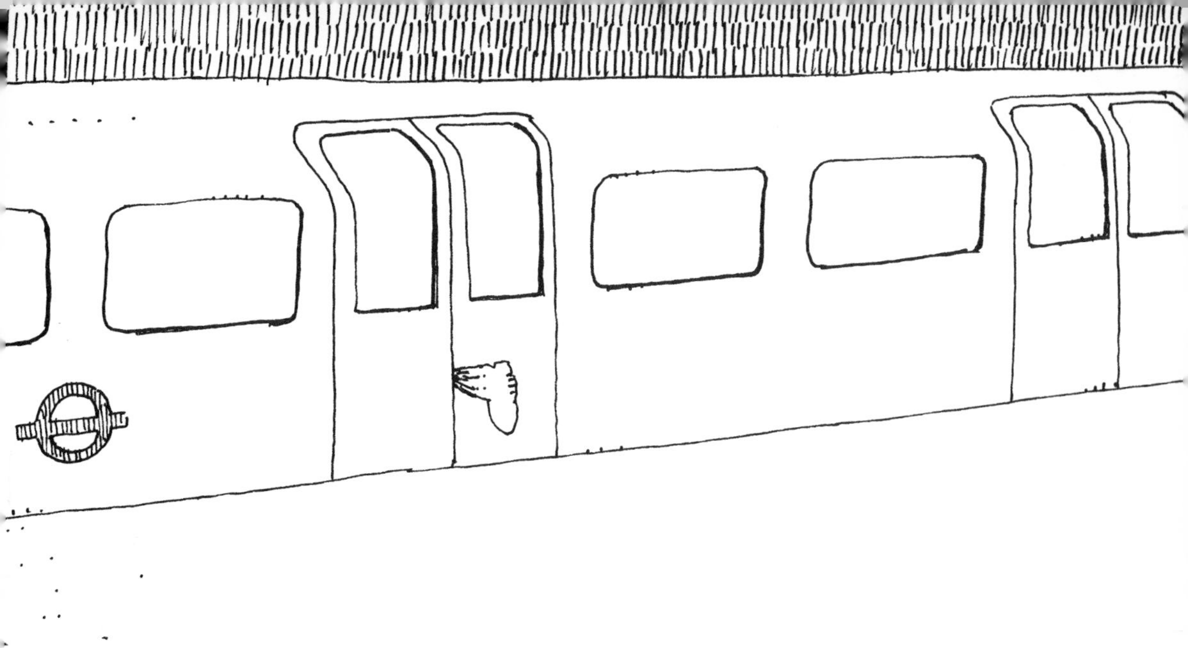

THE HICK FROM THE STICKS

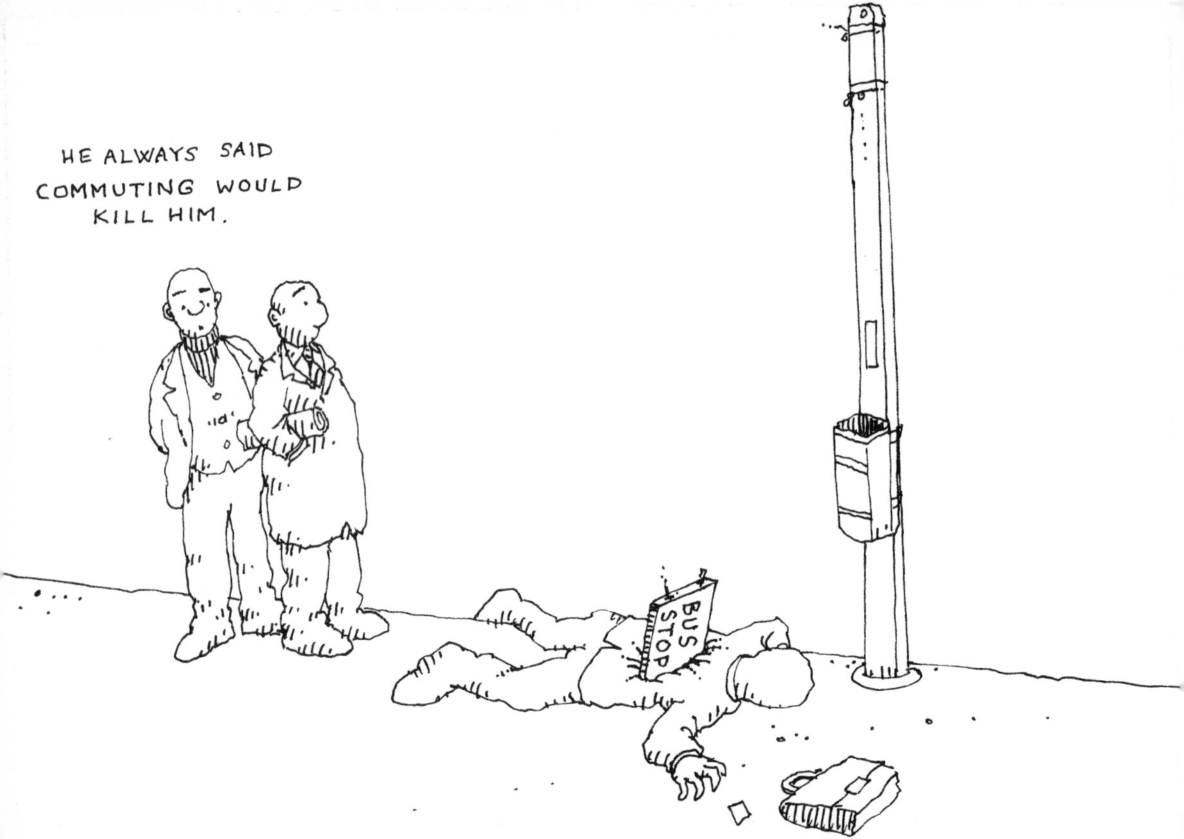
HE ALWAYS SAID COMMUTING WOULD KILL HIM.
BUS STOP

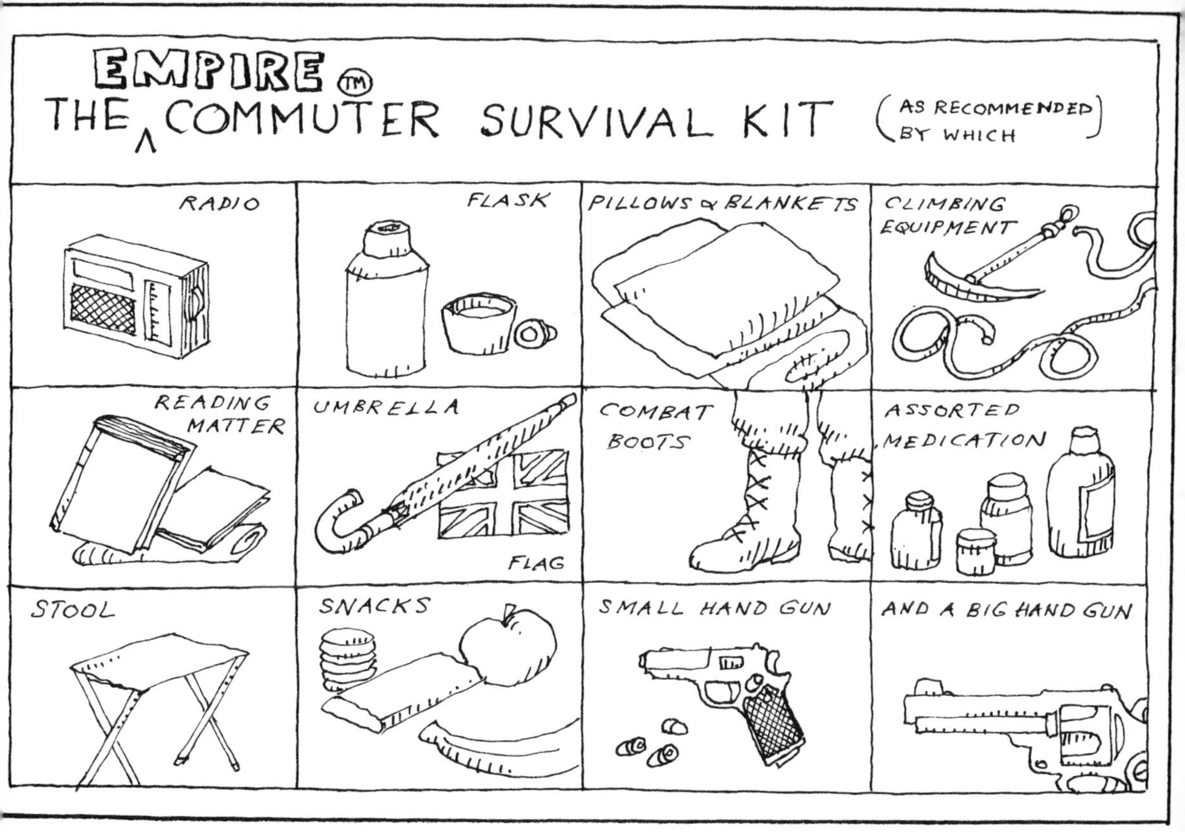
EMPIRE ™
THE COMMUTER SURVIVAL KIT
(AS RECOMMENDED BY WHICH)
RADIO
FLASK
PILLOWS & BLANKETS
CLIMBING EQUIPMENT
READING MATTER
UMBRELLA
FLAG
COMBAT BOOTS
ASSORTED MEDICATION
STOOL
SNACKS
SMALL HAND GUN
AND A BIG HAND GUN

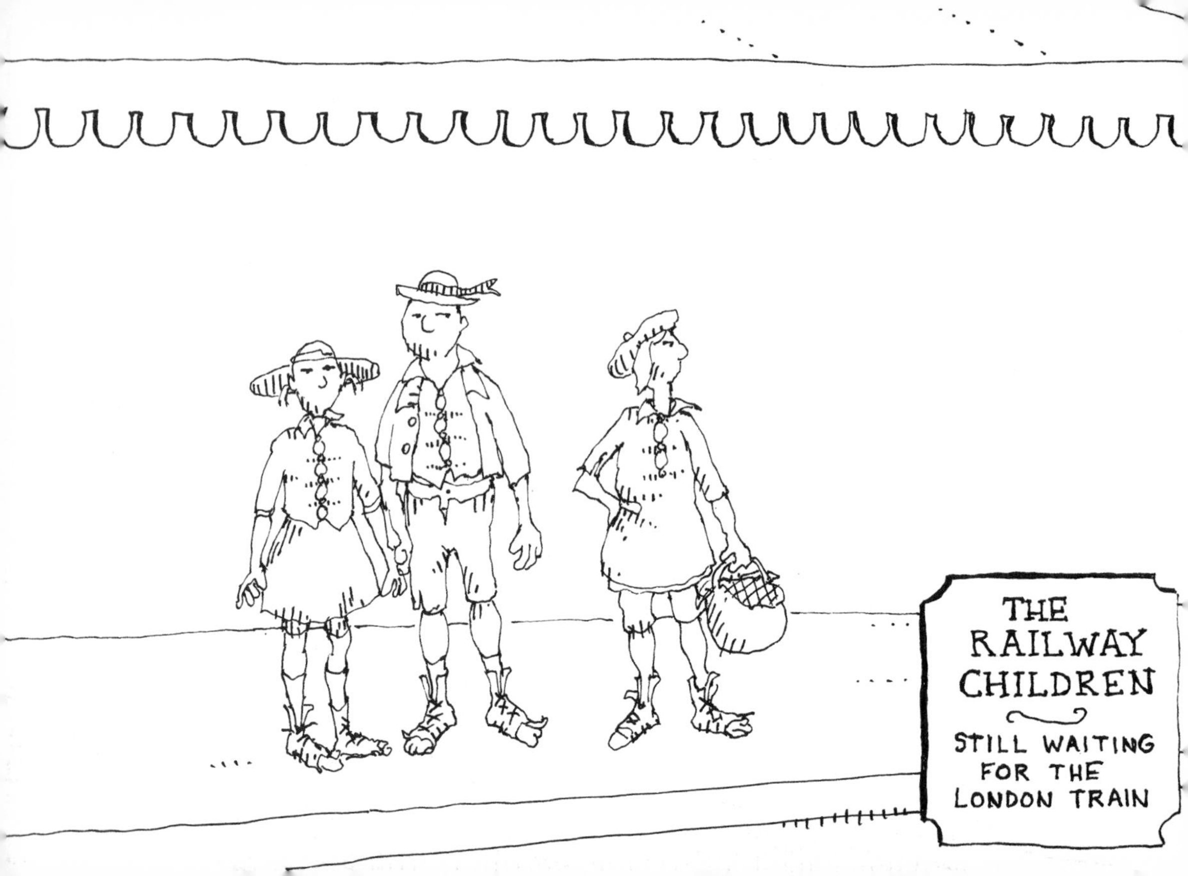
THE RAILWAY CHILDREN
STILL WAITING FOR THE LONDON TRAIN

ERIC MUSGROVE DECIDES TO TAKE A LATER TRAIN

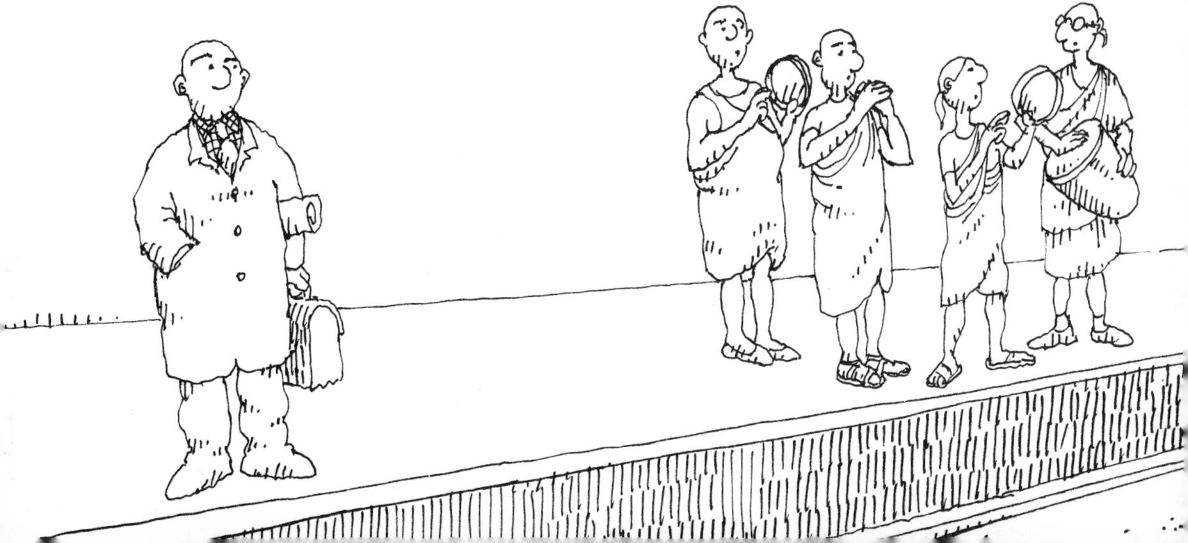

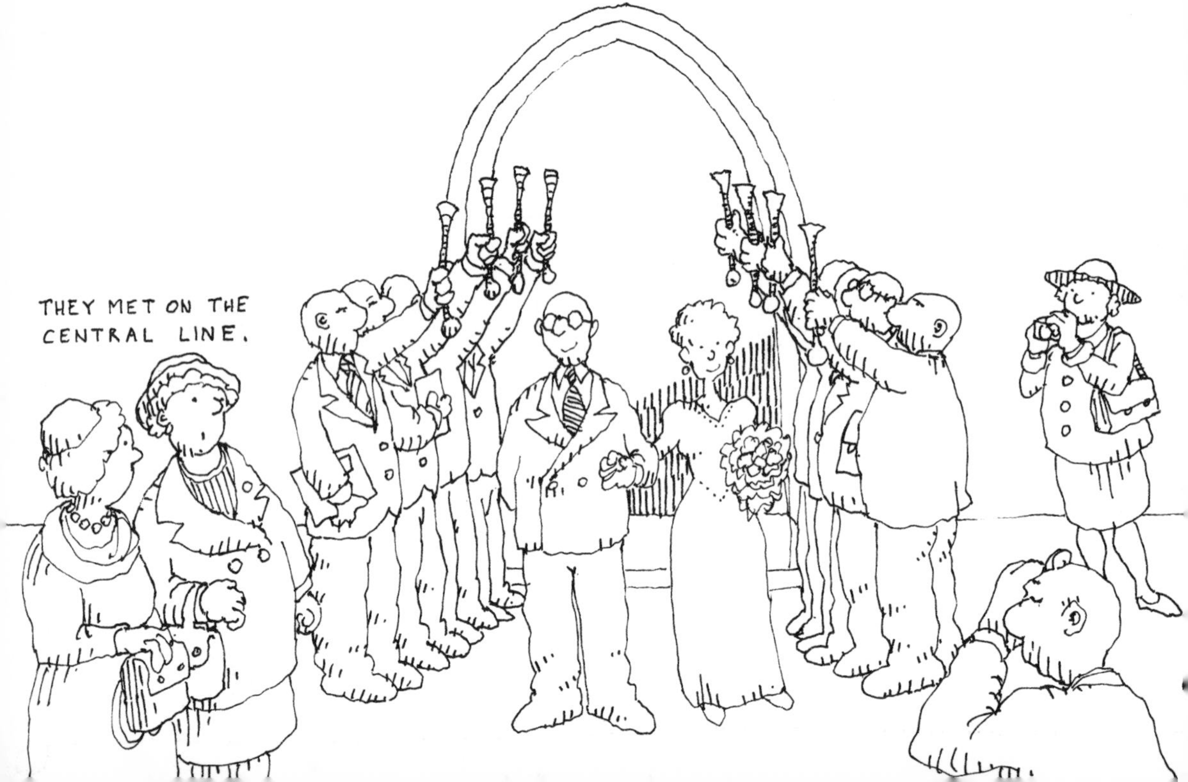

THEY MET ON THE CENTRAL LINE.

# Classic Commuter Cartoons. Number 3

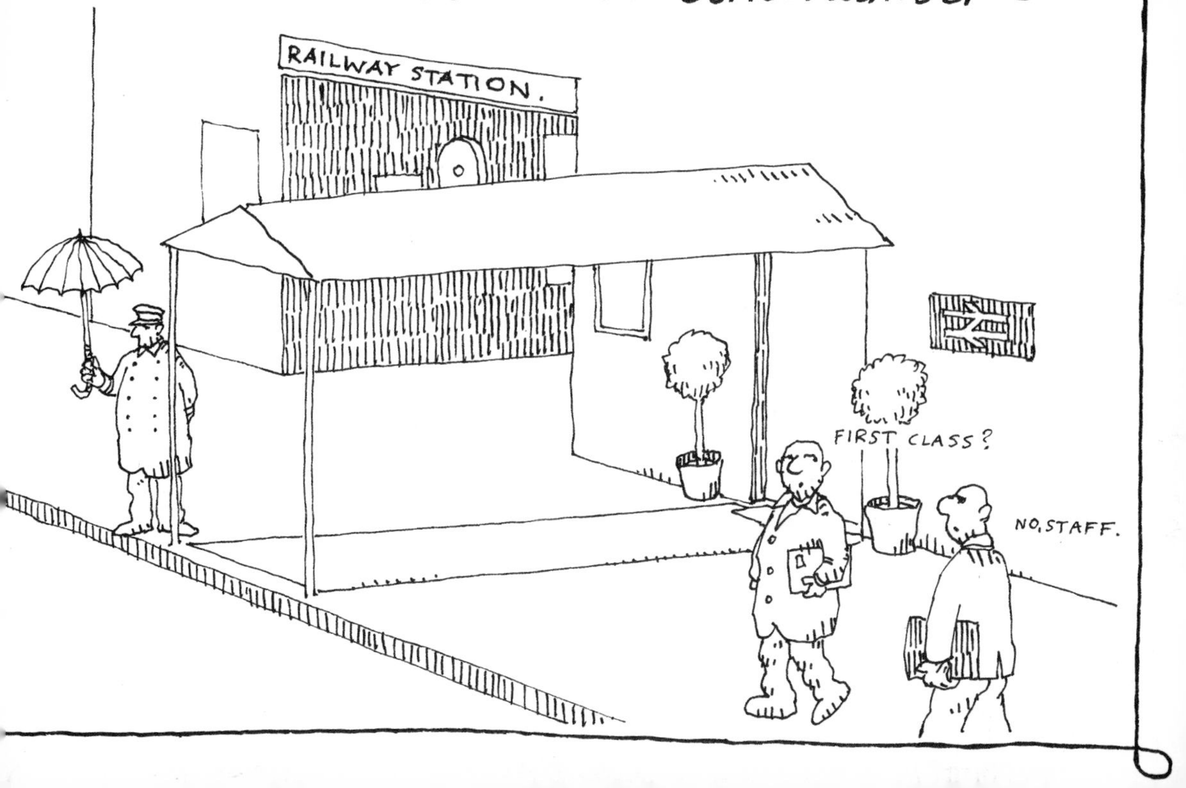
RAILWAY STATION.
FIRST CLASS?
NO. STAFF.

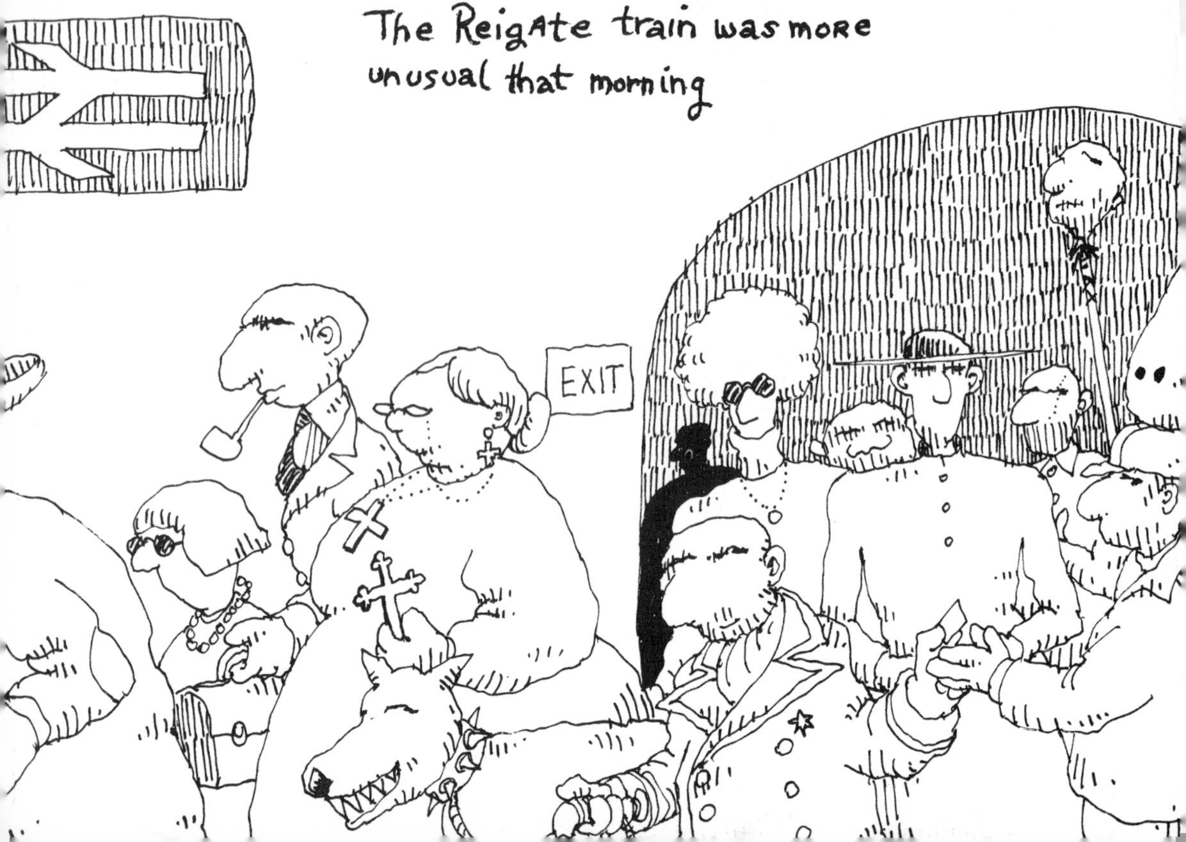
The Reigate train was more unusual that morning
EXIT

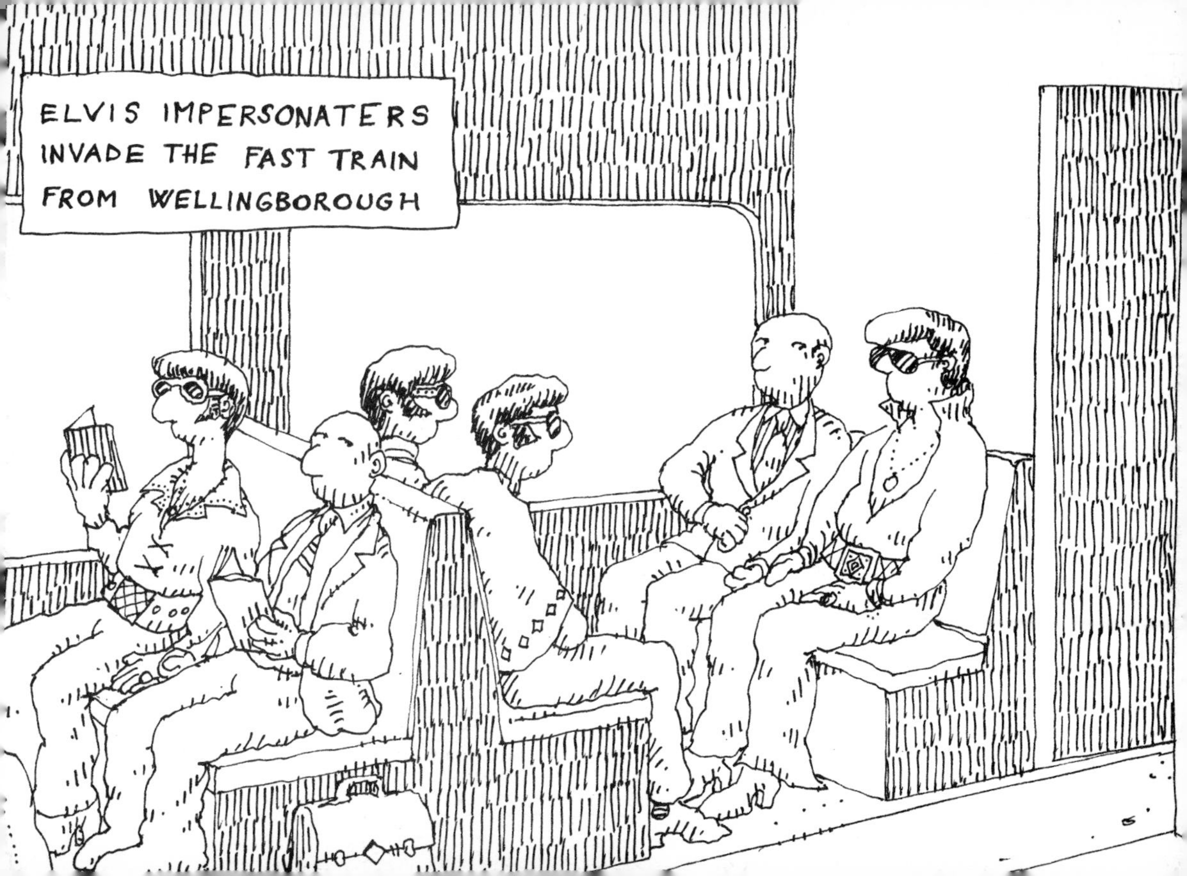
ELVIS IMPERSONATERS
INVADE THE FAST TRAIN
FROM WELLINGBOROUGH

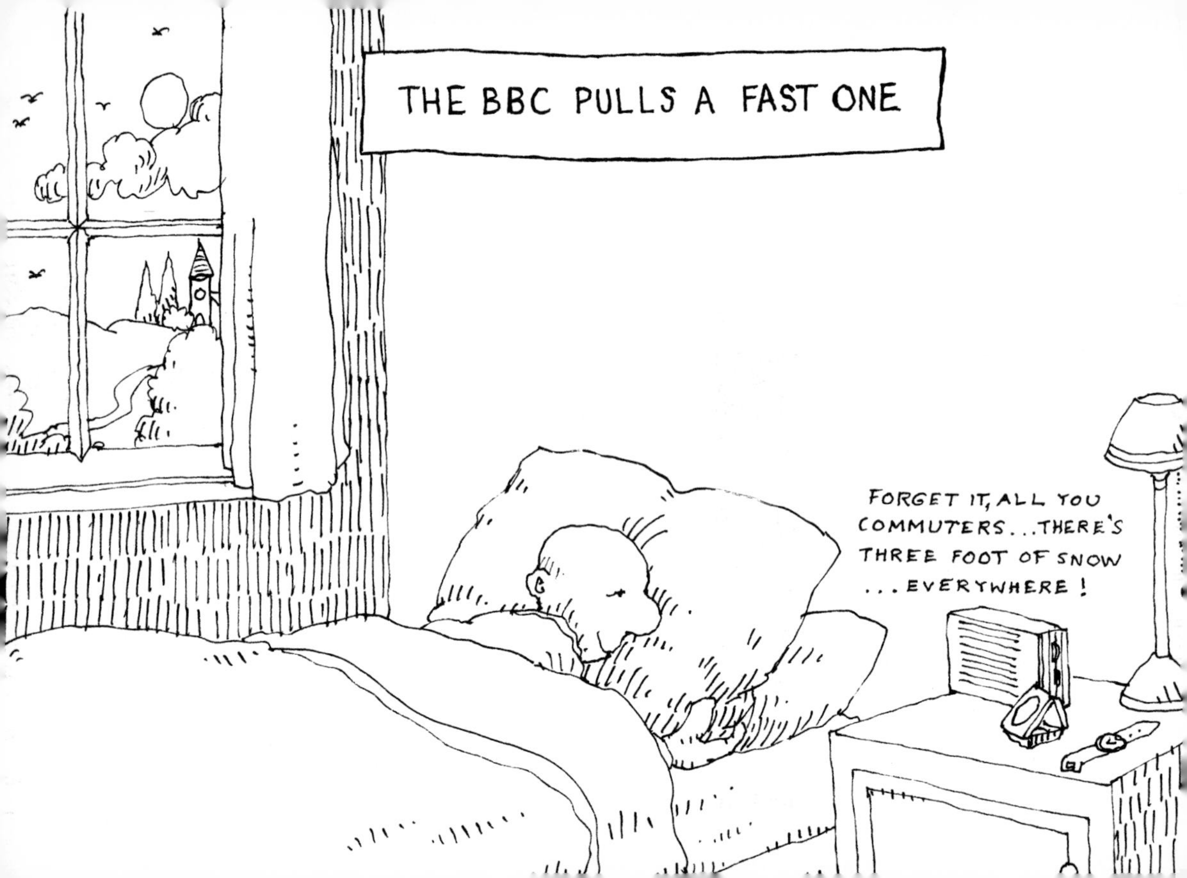
THE BBC PULLS A FAST ONE
FORGET IT, ALL YOU COMMUTERS...THERE'S THREE FOOT OF SNOW ...EVERYWHERE!

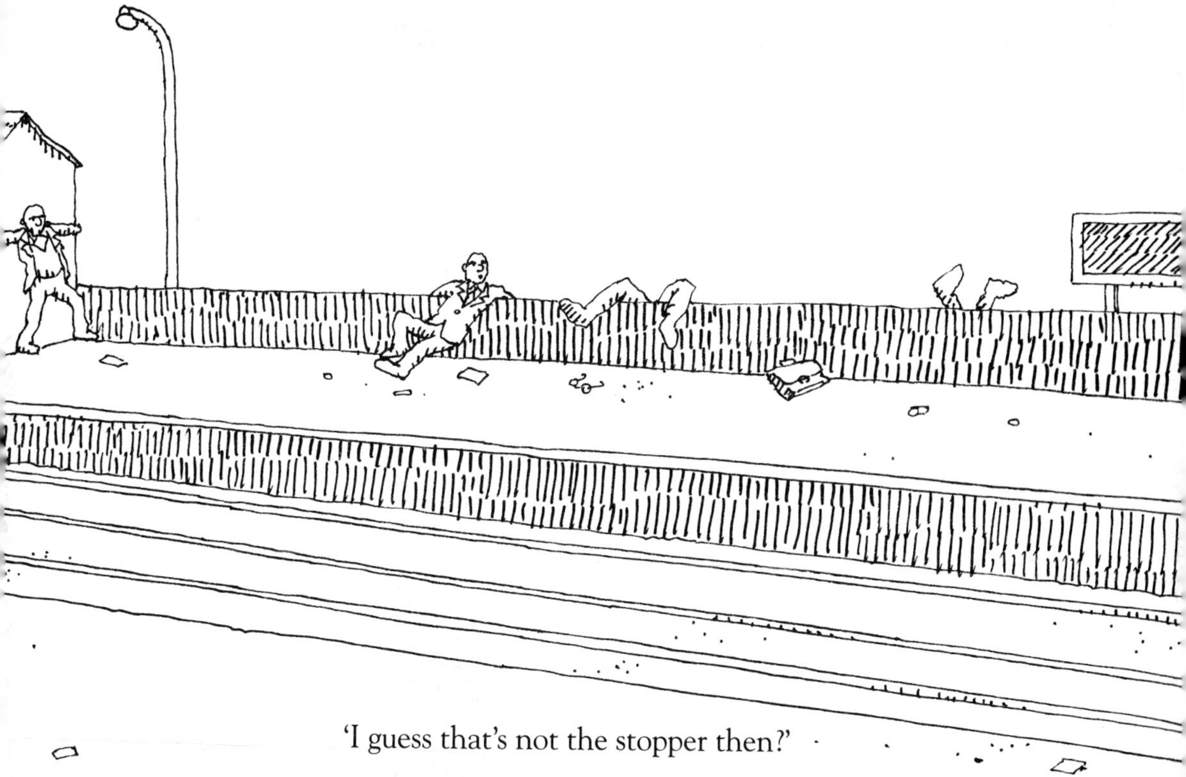

'I guess that's not the stopper then?'

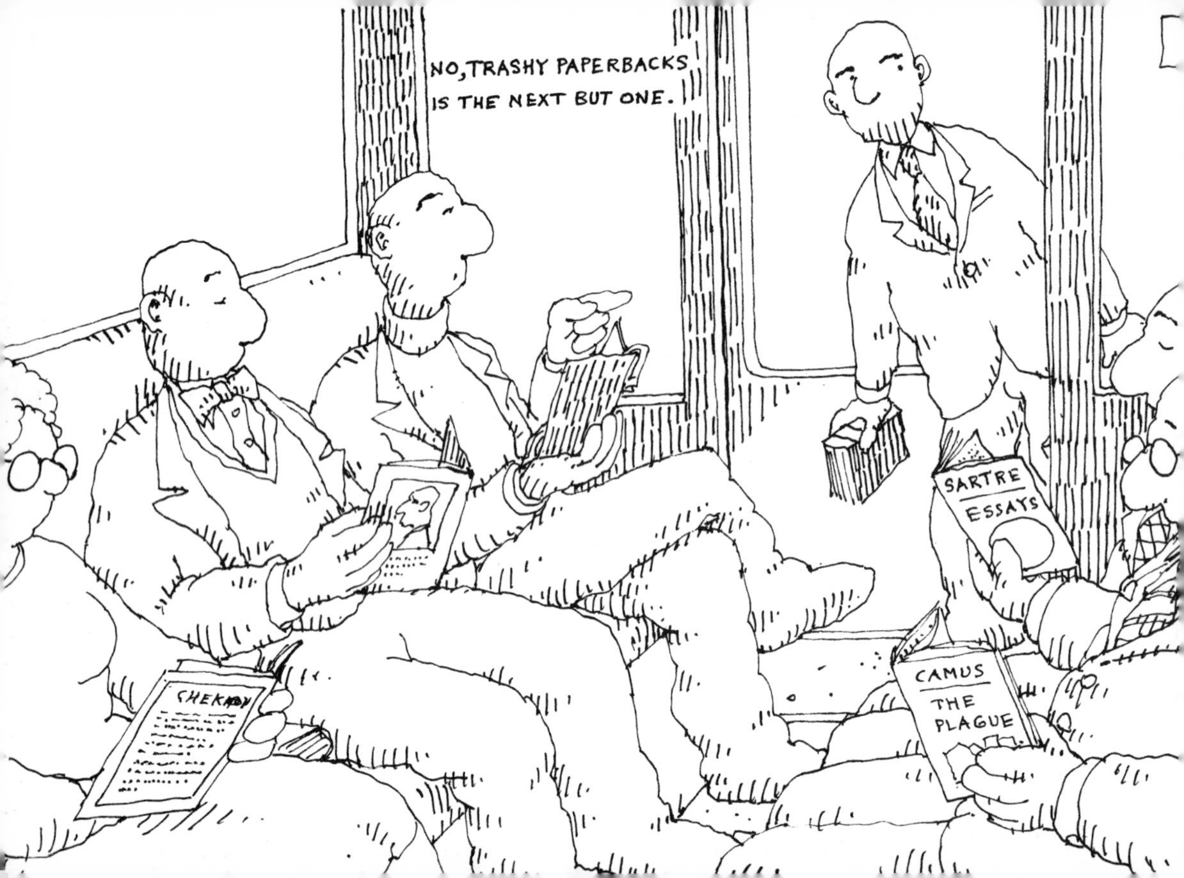
NO, TRASHY PAPERBACKS IS THE NEXT BUT ONE.
SARTRE
ESSAYS
CHEKHOV
CAMUS
THE PLAGUE

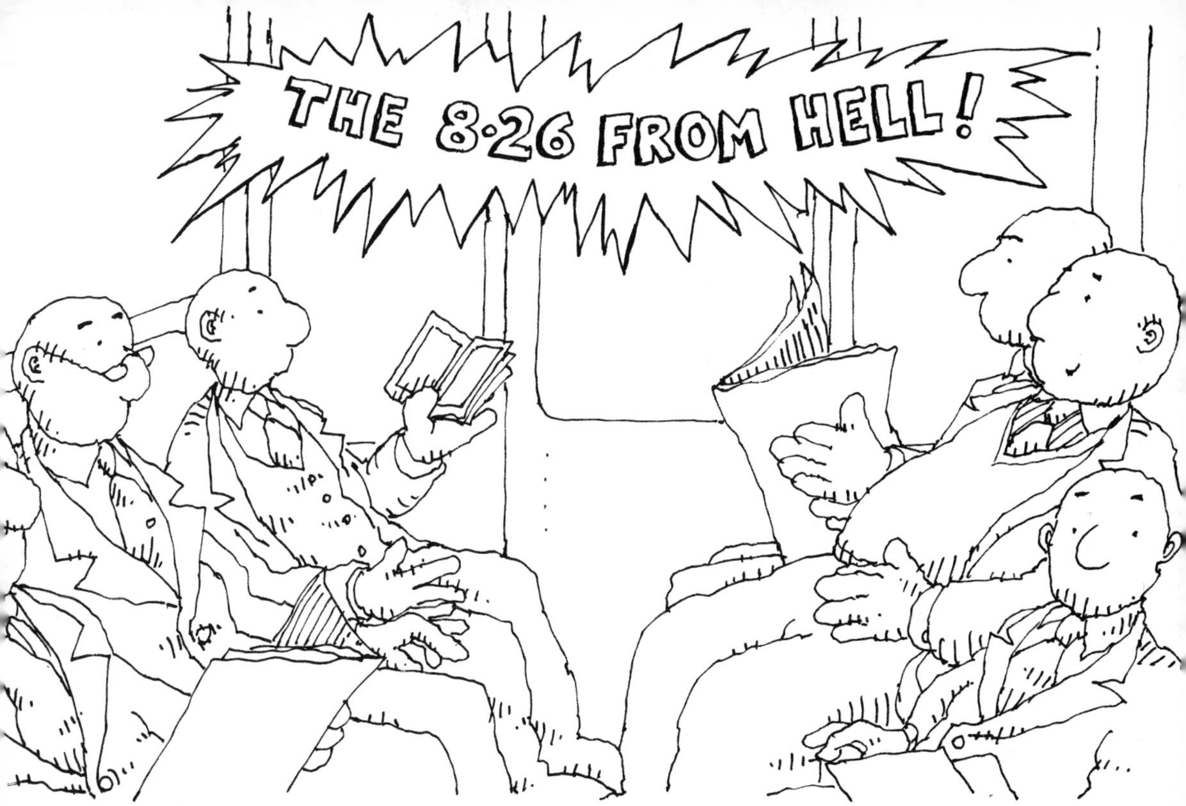
THE 8·26 FROM HELL!

'I don't know about you chaps, but I always get terrible wind after a big Indian lunch.'

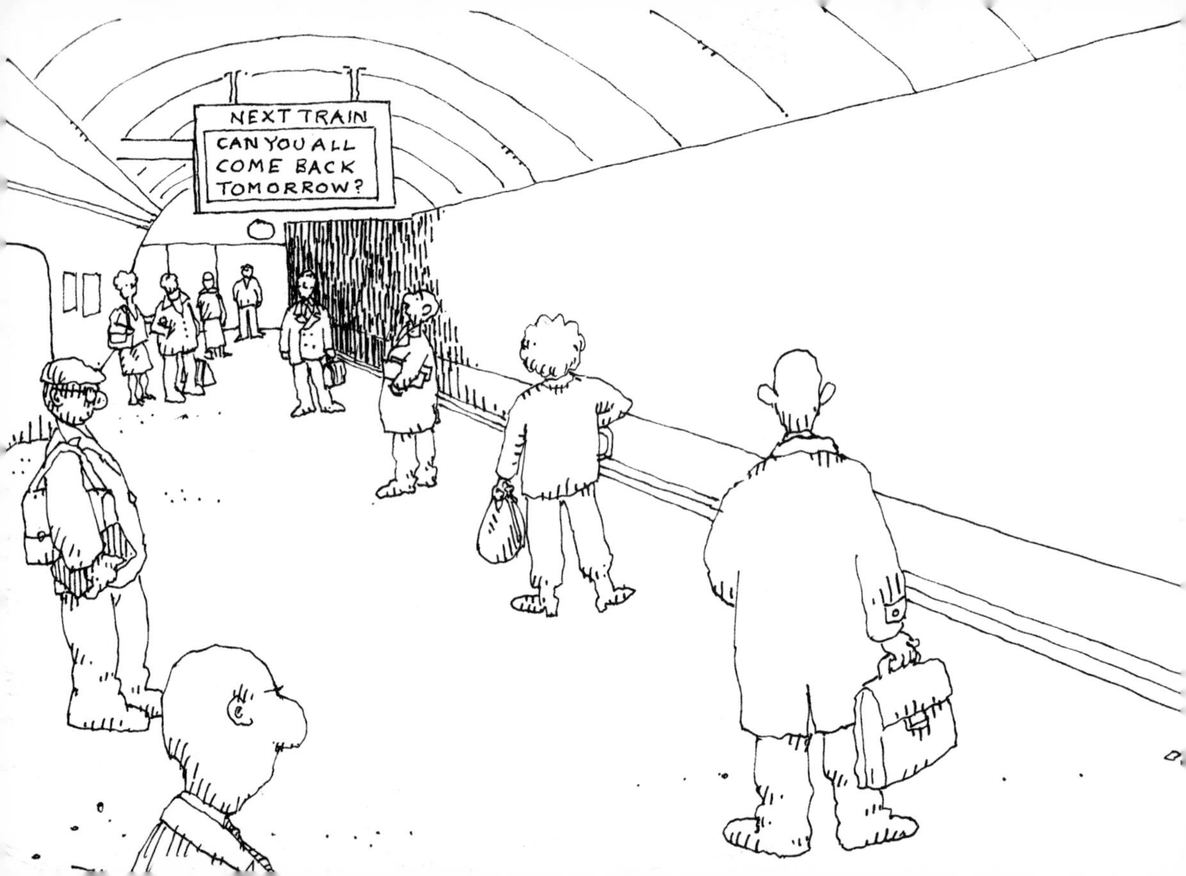
NEXT TRAIN
CAN YOU ALL COME BACK TOMORROW?

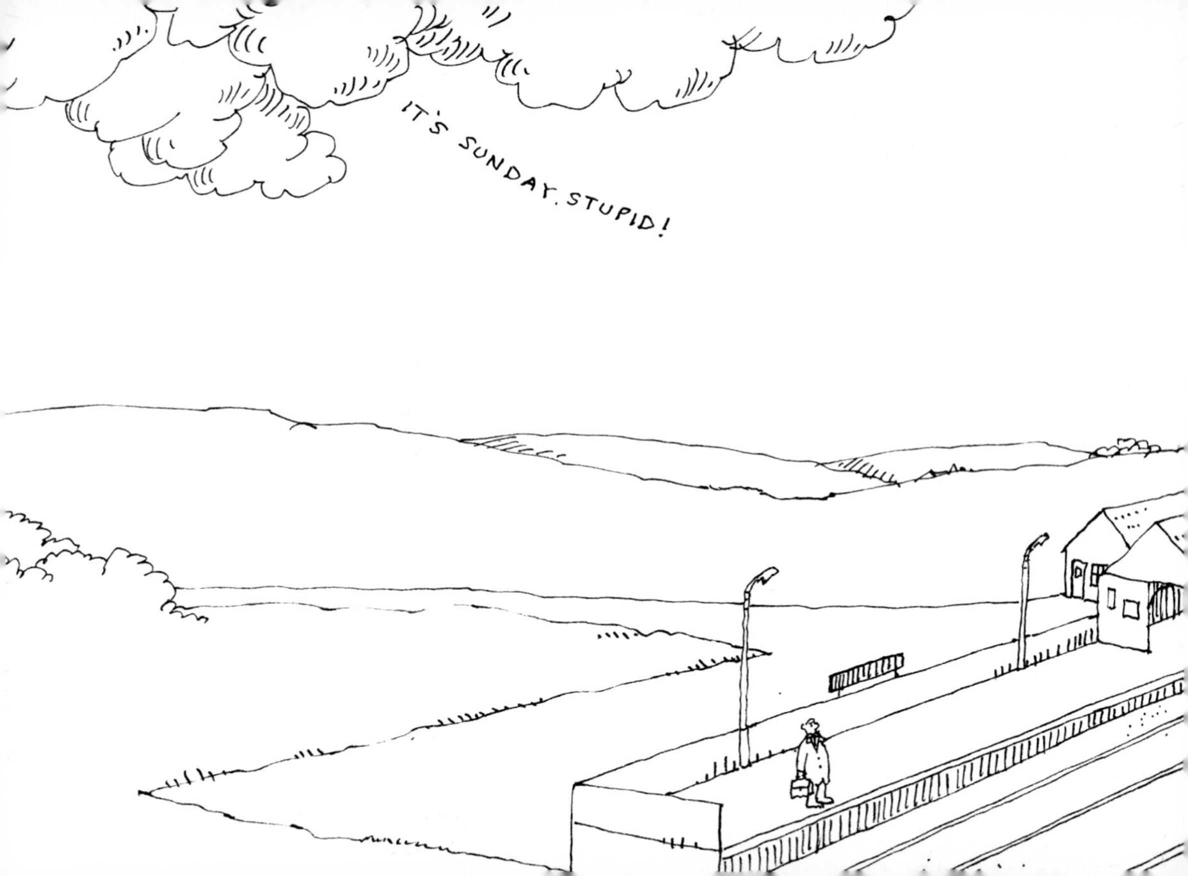
IT'S SUNDAY, STUPID!

AND YOUR CHOSEN SUBJECT IS BRITISH RAIL TICKET CONDITIONS FOR 1989-1990...

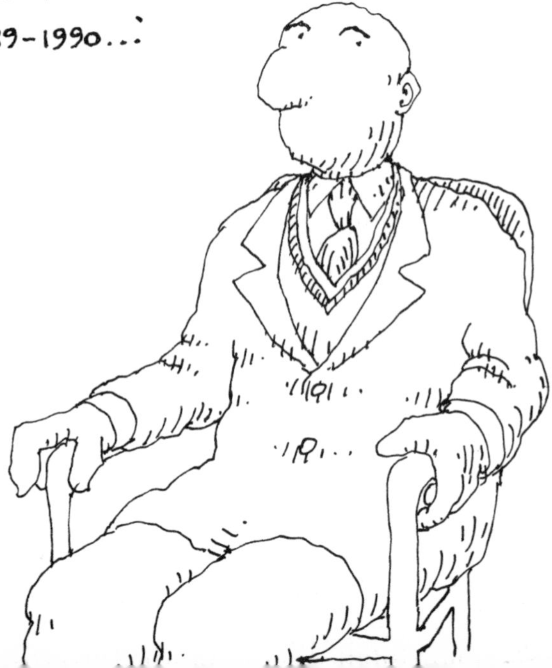

NICE TO SEE TOWNSEND MAKING THE MOST OF HIS SEASON TICKET.

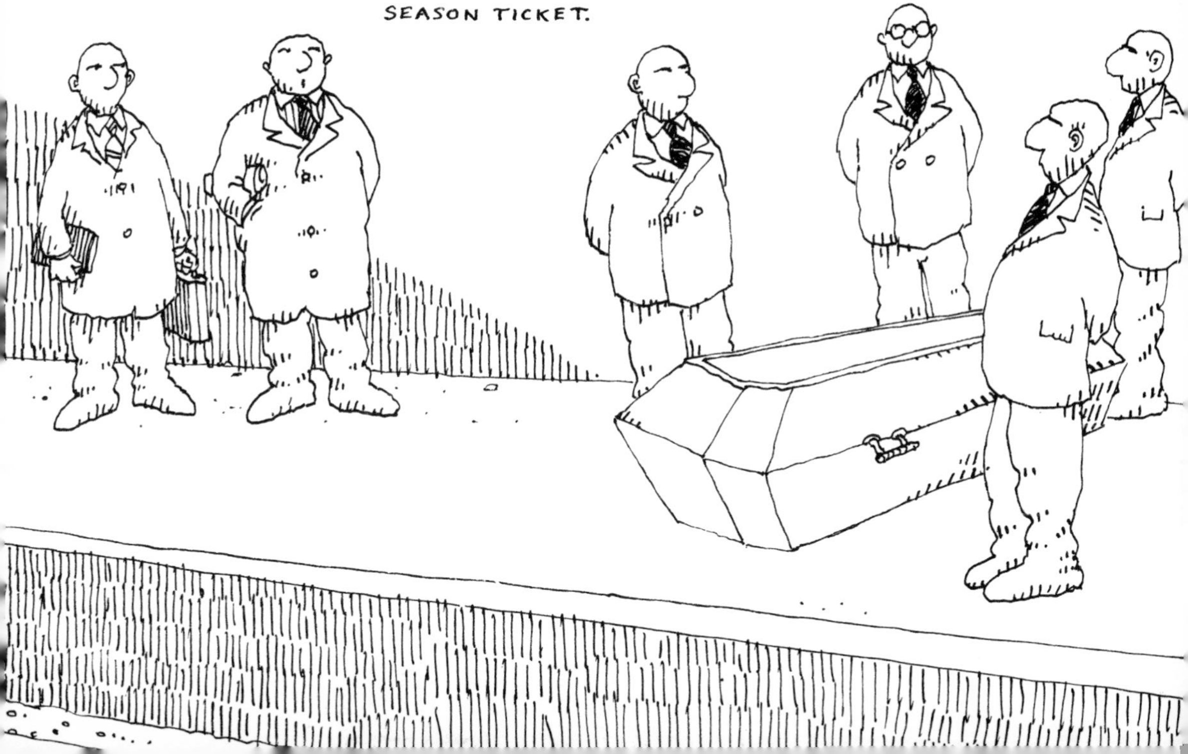

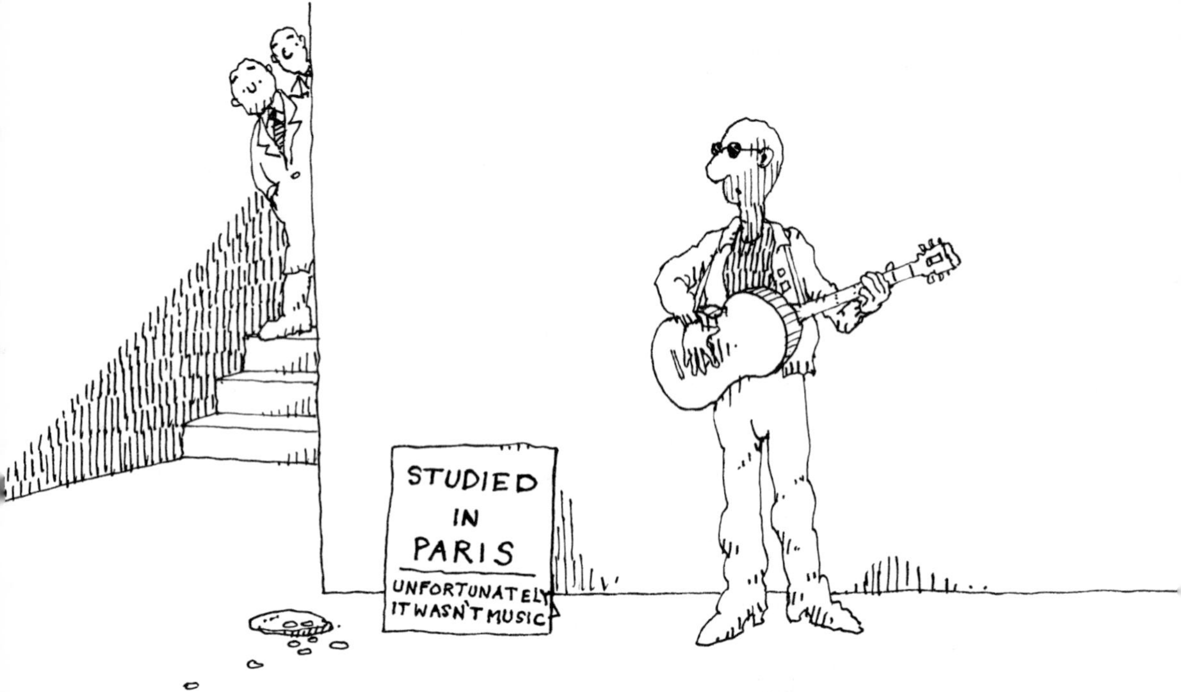
STUDIED
IN
PARIS
UNFORTUNATELY
IT WASN'T MUSIC

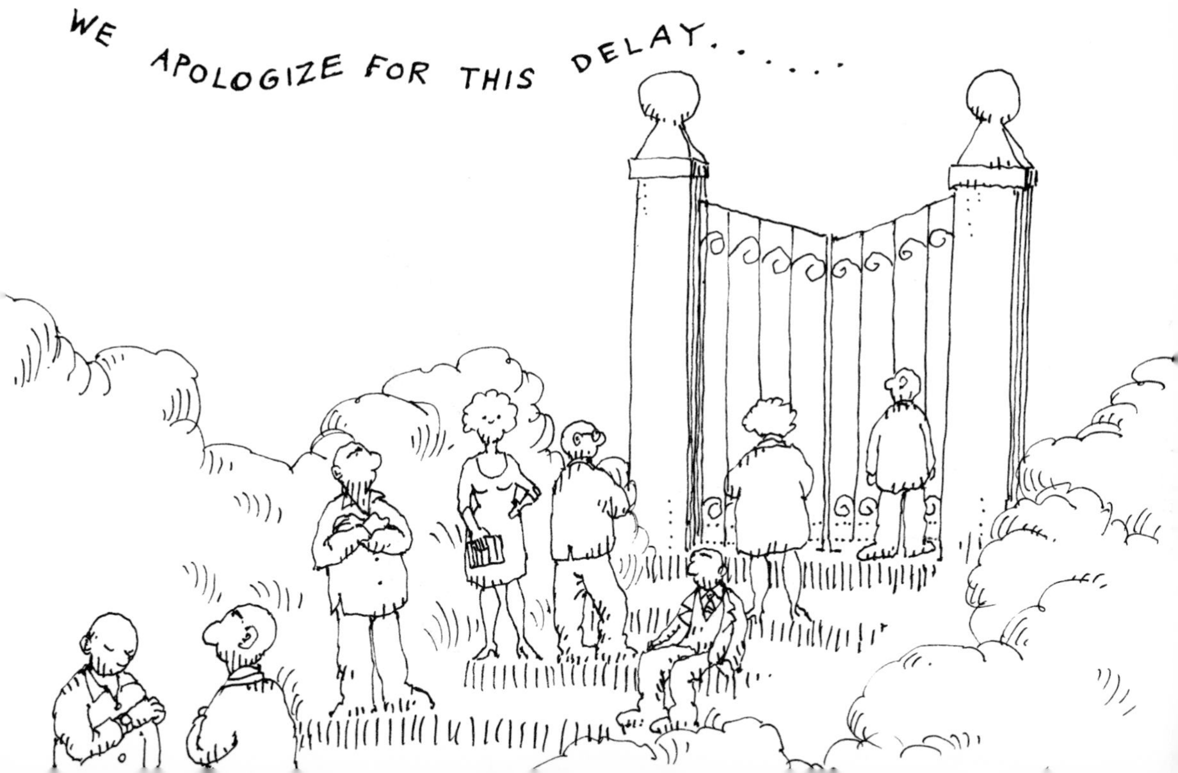
WE APOLOGIZE FOR THIS DELAY......

# MORE HUMOUR TO GET YOU HOME FROM
## SIMON BOND
### AVAILABLE THROUGH ALL GOOD BOOKSELLERS

☐ 101 USES OF A DEAD CAT   £ 4.99 net
The classic!

☐ 101 MORE USES OF A DEAD CAT   £ 3.50 net
The second instalment . . .

☐ DUBIOUS PRACTICES   £ 4.99 net
The world of medicine opened up something rotten

☐ UNIFORMITY   £ 4.95 net
Cartoons on corporals, captains and commanders of all sorts

☐ TEDDY   £ 2.95 net
Everyone's cuddly chum given a good 'going over'

☐ STROKED THROUGH THE COVERS £ 3.95 net
Cricket cartoons for all the fans

☐ TOTALLY U.S.   £ 3.95 net
The very low down on the US of A

☐ ODD DOGS   £ 3.99 net
Man's best friend observed by man's best cartoonist

☐ HOLY UNACCEPTABLE   £ 4.99 net
Riotous religious ribaldry

☐ **If you would like Simon Bond to sign your
copies please tick this box. (Mail orders only)**

**MAIL ORDER FORM** *(Please photocopy this form if you wish)*

• I would like to order the books marked above – please enter the number of copies required in the box to the left of each title.

• I enclose my cheque/P.O. made payable to THE HUMOUR HOUSE for £...... *being the total cost of my order including P & P*
*if applicable.(Postage and packing:* **UK:** *Please add 10% to orders under £20.00, orders over £20.00 post free.* **Overseas:** *Please add 15%)*

*Please charge the total cost of books ordered including P & P if applicable to my Access/Visa * card*

Card No ☐☐☐☐☐☐☐☐☐☐☐☐☐☐☐☐   Expires............Signed ......................

NAME: ...........................................................

ADDRESS: ...........................................................

................................... POST CODE: .................

Please send your order and remittance to:
**HUMOUR BY POST, SILVER LINK PUBLISHING LTD,
THE TRUNDLE, RINGSTEAD ROAD, GREAT ADDINGTON,
KETTERING, NORTHANTS NN14 4BW. TEL/FAX 053678 648**

We endeavour to despatch all orders by return of post but please allow 28 days for delivery. Please note all books are offered subject to availability
and prices and specifications are correct at time of printing (April '92) but are subject to change without notice.   *(* delete as applicable)*

OH, SOD IT, I'LL WALK.

Wallace

678 7422

Family
of
3

2-18-72

reserved.